FORGING THE MIND AND BODY
Advanced Concepts for Martial Artists

By

Chuck Callaway

Copyright © 2020 Chuck Callaway

Cover and illustrations by Chuck Callaway

Pictures by Bryan Callaway

Technical Assistance Conner Callaway

All rights reserved.

ISBN: 9798599458609

Disclaimer and Warning

The martial arts and self-defense involve the use of fighting skills and techniques designed to cause injury to an attacker. The practice and use of these skills can be dangerous and physically demanding. The improper use of any fighting technique could result in both criminal and civil action against the person responsible. Some of the material in this book deals with mental training and exercises for martial arts. It is not intended to replace professional treatment or counseling for persons with behavioral health issues. The information provided in this book is for informational and entertainment purposes only. **The author and publisher are not responsible and assume no liability for any injury that might result from the practice, use, or misuse, of the information contained in this book.** One should always consult a physician before engaging in any physical activity. The information contained in this book is intended to document fighting techniques, skills, principles, and theory as studied and taught by the author to a select few students. While a tremendous amount can be learned from these pages, it is impossible to convey specific movement, subtleties and to correct a student's errors in written form. The reader should seek out a qualified instructor to ensure safe and proper study.

Contents

Introduction..7

Willpower..9

Visualization...19

Mind Clearing...27

Breathing...35

Explosive Power...56

Adapt and Flow..69

The Point of No Return...............................88

Sensitivity..92

Tension/Sealing the Gates........................111

Conquering Fear......................................122

The Checkers Principle.............................129

Controlling the Ego..................................146

Psychological Strategy.............................151

Resistance...158

Reaction Without Thought……………………………….172

Conclusion………………………………………………………..178

About the Author…………………………………………….. 179

Acknowledgments

My deepest thanks to my beautiful wife Laura for her support and for being my soul mate!

Introduction

The mind is an incredible tool that is often overlooked by martial artists in their daily training. In our modern world it is easy to get wrapped up in the technical aspects of our training and forget to dedicate the necessary time to developing skills that go beyond the physical. The purpose of this book is to show you how to take your martial arts training to a much higher level. One that does not rely on physical skill alone, but instead unifies the mind and body into an unstoppable machine.

I have been blessed in my life to have studied martial arts with numerous masters who not only stressed physical fighting skills, but also the vital importance of the mind. These skills were never presented to me as mystical or magical, but rather as the glue that holds your physical art together. Without the skills I will present to you in this book, my martial art would simply be a hollow shell, with very little deeper value.

The great beauty of this knowledge is that it benefits you far beyond self-defense or being able to fight. It carries over into your daily life and provides you with skills to deal with any obstacles that life throws your way. Once these skills are mastered, you will be able to clear your mind in an instant, make tough decisions, lead others, adapt and respond to change, and calm yourself in times of extreme stress.

You will notice the benefits of these skills start to appear in other areas of your life. Maybe when you are public speaking or playing a sport. Others will also notice a positive change in your mental attitude and behavior. The irony is that the more you develop the concepts in this book, the less you will need physical fighting techniques in your life. As you grow older, nature takes back what's hers. You will start to lose your physical attributes such as speed, power, and endurance no matter how much you train. But like a fine scotch, the concepts, and skills you will discover within this book only get better with time. I hope you enjoy the journey.

Chuck Callaway
January 2021

Willpower

Willpower is the ability to persevere and keep going despite all odds. Having the determination to accomplish a task with the mindset that nothing will stop you from achieving your goals is a powerful tool for both self-defense and daily life. To a warrior, willpower is an incredible asset that has throughout history, turned the tides of battles. To a martial artist, willpower will give you the ability to keep fighting and survive, even when injured and in significant pain. In many cases, willpower can bring out inner strengths that we didn't know we possessed.

We have all heard the stories of the mother who somehow finds the strength to lift a car off of her child following a horrific traffic accident. Or the desperate prisoner who somehow manages to break his handcuffs and escape. In times of great stress, the human body is capable of remarkable things. But how can willpower be developed? How are we able to summon up this ability at will? Are there ways to build your own willpower to a much higher level?

Developing your willpower can be done, but it isn't easy. It requires hard work and constant dedication. The very nature of increasing your willpower requires you to push yourself beyond your current capabilities. Before we delve into the ways to improve your willpower, let me introduce you to your number one enemy when it comes to willpower.

The Voice In your Head

Your number one enemy when it comes to building your willpower is the voice in your head. That subconscious voice that will try to convince you that you have had enough or it's time to quit. The voice that provides you with excuse after excuse for why you don't need to push forward and complete the task at hand. If your willpower was Batman, then this voice is the Joker! Centuries ago, people often believed that this inner voice was the Devil or a demon trying to get you to commit sins. Don't underestimate the voice inside of your head because it is incredibly strong. If you don't control it, it will control you.

Take a moment and think about the last time your inner voice convinced you that you should do something contrary to your goals. Maybe you had gone months without a drink of alcohol and the voice talked you in to having that one little drink that then turned into several. Maybe you had bills to pay but the voice convinced you that it was ok to spend your money on something you wanted rather than something you needed. Usually, we feel bad or guilty after falling victim to the voice. The good news is the voice is a part of you. You can control it and actually make it work for you.

How do we train the inner voice to be positive and convince you to stay the course and accomplish your goals rather than disrupt your progress? The first step is to create a second inner voice. One that is much more powerful and positive than the negative voice. The new positive voice will have two jobs. First it will be responsible for overriding and controlling the negative voice. Second, it will be your internal support mechanism. When you feel like you can't continue or it is pointless to try, your new inner voice will be the drill sergeant that makes you push on. Let's start.

Willpower Exercise One
Create the Positive Voice

Find a quiet place to sit down and relax. Close your eyes, breathe deep, and release all tension in your body. Keep your mind clear and don't fall asleep. Very soon the negative voice will appear. It may be subtle at first and you might not recognize right away that it is there. Soon the voice will become louder. It will try to convince you to do something else, maybe something more fun. It will try to distract you from what you are working to accomplish by reminding you of other things you could be doing.

Once you recognize the voice is present, capture it. Imagine that you now have control of the voice and are locking it in a prison cell. Imagine that a new voice has been born to replace the negative one. The new voice is strong and positive. It is much more powerful than the old voice.

From now on, anytime the old voice chimes in with negativity, or tempts you to stray from your goals, the new voice takes over and keeps you on track. Once you recognize the strong presence of the new voice, ingrain it in your mind and end this exercise. Repeat this exercise daily until you feel the positive voice is ever present, keeping the negative voice under control.

The obvious goal of this mental exercise is to develop a more positive and stronger subconscious thought pattern that will help you stay focused and obtain your goals. Keep in mind that negative thoughts are very easy to acquire and often difficult to look past. After you master this exercise, you will start to have more positive thought patterns. When negative thoughts occur, your stronger, positive subconscious will control and suppress them.

A word of caution though. Don't mistake common sense for negative thoughts. If your inner voice tells you something is wrong, don't just ignore and suppress it. There may be times when you need to listen to the negative voice, but ultimately you have control. Now that you have developed a positive inner voice, let's build your willpower to the next level.

Go Beyond Quitting

Now we will start the actual process of building your willpower. The purpose of this exercise is to develop in you the drive to always go above and beyond what is required. To understand the concept of this exercise, imagine a weightlifter bench pressing weights in the gym. His spotter is standing behind the bench providing verbal support. As the weightlifter starts to finish his final repetition of lifts, the spotter yells at him to push out one more repetition. "Come on, let's go, one more, you can do it!" This is the exact mentality you want to foster within yourself. When the negative voice says you are done, your positive voice takes over and you take it one step further.

Willpower Exercise Two
Standing Training

An excellent method of developing willpower and the ability to go beyond quitting is standing training. Many internal martial arts systems use this exercise and link it to the development of internal energy, chi power, and other mystical skills. I personally believe that the original reason for this type of training was to develop willpower and physical strength in the body.

The perfect example of this is the Chinese martial art of Xing Yi Quan that was classically taught to the Chinese army. Holding a standing posture for extended periods of time is a key training component of this fighting system. Understanding that willpower is one of the most important skills a warrior can possess for the battlefield, it makes perfect sense to train them in a system that quickly cultivates willpower, rather than focusing on an esoteric chi building method. In fact, Xing Yi Quan is commonly translated to mean Form-**Will**-Boxing in English.

The practice of standing training with a focus on developing willpower can be done almost anywhere. First, you will need some sort of a timer. I use a three-dollar egg timer I purchased at the local grocery store. There are also various stopwatch apps available for mobile devices that can be used. You will want to start off slow by standing for only about two minutes at a time. You will gradually increase the time you stand as your strength and willpower improve. Regardless of claims that you must stand for an hour or more, I believe that you can adequately improve your willpower by standing for no more than fifteen minutes a day.

Once you have located a quiet spot to stand, and have a timer available, you will assume a specific standing posture. Which posture you choose to use is not really important, as long as it puts a slight degree of strain on the body when held. I like to use the primary Xing Yi Quan posture because it is fairly simple and serves a martial arts function. This posture is called the trinity Posture or San Ti.

To assume the trinity posture, stand with your right foot forward approximately shoulders width apart. The right foot points straight ahead and the rear foot is turned at a forty-five-degree angle. The knees are slightly bent, and the heels of the feet are on the same line. Your right arm is extended with your elbow bent and your fingers slightly spread. The index finger is in line with your nose. The left hand is held near your waistline with the fingers slightly spread and the thumb touching your stomach. Your shoulders are curved, and your chin is slightly tucked. Relax the entire body in this position. Don't worry about holding the posture perfectly or feeling energy or anything of that nature. Remember the goal is to develop our willpower.

Set your timer for two minutes and assume the Trinity posture. Keep your mind clear and don't move until the timer goes off. When you hear the sound of the timer, continue to hold the posture for a few extra seconds before you stop. If you have never practiced standing before, you will experience discomfort. Your legs may start to shake or cramp as you stand. The inner voice will no doubt try to convince you to stop but don't listen. Your strong inner voice will have you push on beyond the ring of the timer.

As the timer ticks down, your level of discomfort will increase. The negative inner voice will provide you with many excuses to quit but suppress those thoughts and instead, listen to the new positive voice which is stronger. When the timer goes off, continue to hold the posture. Reinforce in your mind that nothing can stop you. You never give up. How long you continue to stand after the time expires is irrelevant. The important thing is that you push past the finish line.

After a while it will become much easier to stand in the trinity posture for fifteen minutes. When this is no longer a challenge to you and your willpower is not being pushed to the limit, instead of increasing the time, change or modify the posture you use. You can start by standing on only one leg in the trinity posture. You might also want to assume the classic horse stance with your legs bent almost horizontal with the ground. Instead of standing in a posture for hours on end, use a more challenging posture to accomplish your goals in a shorter time frame. The below photos show the postures you can use for this exercise.

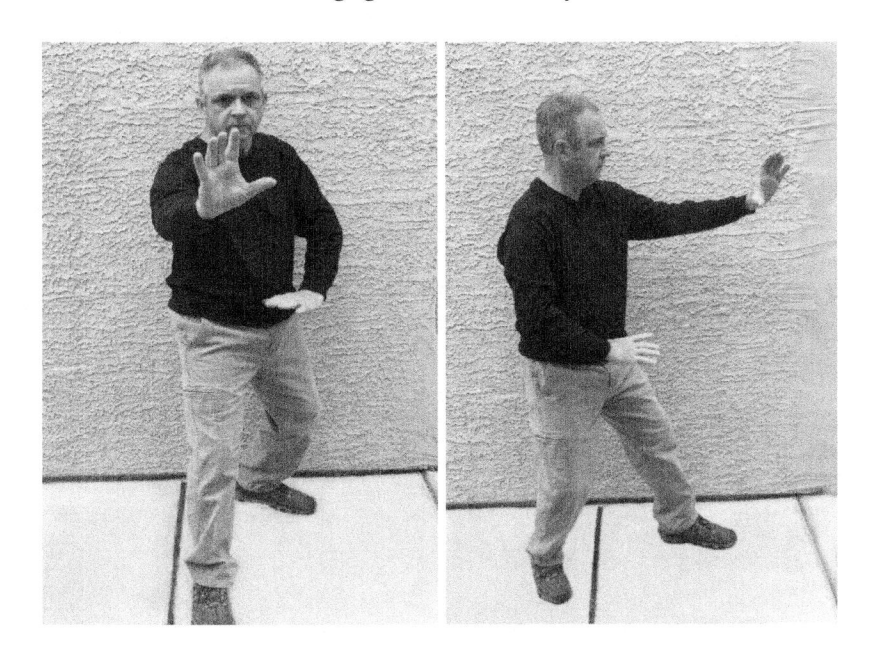

The Trinity Posture (front and side view)

The trinity posture (on one leg)

The classic horse stance

Willpower Verses Chi Power

You can't have a conversation on standing training without sliding down the rabbit hole of chi power. My goal in this book is to provide you with proven effective methods to take your fighting skills to a higher level. Willpower is a tangible skill to develop that is critical in a real life or death encounter. Chi power on the other hand, is a controversial subject that is not within the scope of this book.

Although I believe that we all have an intrinsic energy in our bodies, whether or not it can be used for fighting is open to debate. As you study the standing training exercise, don't get caught up in the idea of developing chi power that is often intertwined with this exercise. I think of it like this, chi power is the leprechaun's pot of gold and willpower is your paycheck. You can spend your life searching for the pot of gold at the end of the rainbow, but when the bills come due, you're going to rely on that paycheck to save your rear end. If you happen to stumble upon the pot of gold while you are traveling along your path, well then you have the luck of the Irish!

Willpower Exercise Three
Cold Turkey

This is probably the most difficult exercise you can do to build your willpower because it is actually much more than just a simple exercise. In this exercise, you build your willpower by actually using it. Just like the muscles in your body become stronger with use, your willpower will become stronger the more you employ it. I'm sure you have heard the saying that to learn how to swim, you must get in the water. For this exercise we are getting in the water! You will pick a habit that you wish to eliminate and simply stop cold turkey.

Take a moment to think about your daily routine in life. What is there about your day-to-day lifestyle that you would like to eliminate? I suggest starting with the low hanging fruit. For example, if you have smoked three packs of cigarettes a day for twenty years, maybe you don't want to start off with this as your goal for the cold turkey exercise. Instead pick something easier to obtain, such as cutting out junk food, or saving a few dollars extra each month by eliminating the fancy coffee you drink. Once you identify the target for the cold turkey exercise, quit. Stop doing the habit you want to break.

Keep a journal to track your progress and count the days you have gone without engaging in the habitual behavior you chose to eliminate. Depending on the type of habit you are dealing with, actual physical withdrawals might occur. You may feel like something is missing and there is a void to fill to replace it. If this feeling occurs, replace the old bad habit with a new positive one. If you used to have a giant soda at noon every day, replace it with a glass of juice, or maybe even a jog around the block. As time goes by, your urges to engage in the old behavior will diminish. Your willpower becomes stronger.

Although the cold turkey exercise is aimed at eliminating unwanted behavior, it can also be used to develop your willpower to do a new behavior such as working out every day. Just like adding more weights to a barbell when your muscles strengthen, target tougher habits as your willpower strengthens. This exercise can truly change your life if taken seriously.

Remember that building your willpower is not easy. It takes a tremendous amount of effort and self determination to break bad habits and develop a strong willpower. You will fail along the way, but when you do, don't give up. Ironically, if you keep pushing forward even when you fail, you are still developing your willpower. Once your willpower is strong, there is literally nothing that you can't accomplish.

Visualization

Visualization is a powerful tool that all martial artists should add to their training. The beauty of visualization practice is that it can be done anywhere from the top of a mountain to the back of a taxicab. By incorporating visualization exercises into your life, you can stay sharp when physical practice is impossible.

What is Visualization?

Visualization is simply using the mind's eye to picture or visualize different scenarios and outcomes. It could be seen as harnessing the power of your imagination and using it to get real results in your physical performance. This is not some new age wish and it will happen spiritual practice, but rather a scientifically proven method that can be used to enhance your skills.

In the early nineties I attended a seminar that was put on by a very well-respected martial artist. During the seminar he spoke about the power of visualization and talked about a study that was done at a major university. The study involved dart players who were separated into two groups. The first group actually practiced throwing darts every day for an hour while the second group only visualized themselves throwing darts for the same period of time. At the conclusion of the study, the group that only visualized themselves throwing darts consistently scored more bullseyes than the group that actually threw darts.

I have also heard the story of a gifted piano player who was sent to prison for political reasons. While in prison, he did not have access to a piano and could only visualize himself practicing while in his cell. Eventually after years, he was released and asked to perform. He played with such skill that many people said it was his best performance ever, despite not touching a piano for years. His only method of practice was visualization.

The basic idea behind visualization is that the human brain cannot differentiate between actual physical practice and mental visualization of practice. Essentially you can trick the mind into believing that you are experiencing a real physical activity, which then conditions the physical body to react and perform.

I have noticed in my own visualization training that my muscles will twitch, and I can actually feel a response in my body as I visualize certain techniques being performed. This phenomenon is very similar to when you are asleep, and your body suddenly jerks while dreaming that you are falling or fighting someone. Let's look at a few visualization exercises that will enhance your physical skills.

Visualization Exercise One
Your Mental Dojo

Find a quiet location where you won't be disturbed. You may sit on a chair or lie down as long as you are comfortable and won't fall asleep during the exercise. Close your eyes, breathe deep and relax your body. As you engage in any visualization exercise, try to see the mental picture as vividly as possible in your mind's eye. Just like you have a physical location for your training, we will now establish your mental training area.

Imagine you are standing at the base of a mountain. The cold wind nips at your body, giving you a chill as you slowly climb an ancient stone pathway that leads up the sheer cliff edge of the mountain. As you get closer to the peak, a doorway suddenly comes into view, carved right into the side of the mountain. Large iron rings serve as handles on the twenty-foot-tall doors made from ancient wood. You firmly grasp the rings with both hands and pull the heavy doors open.

Warm air engulfs your body as you step into the rock carved passageway. You immediately see that a short distance ahead, the tunnel opens into a large room. As you make your way through the tunnel towards the room, you are calm and comfortable because you realize you have been to this place before. It is familiar to you because it is yours, and yours only. The tunnel opens into a very large room that is filled with every type of training apparatus known to man. This room is your mental dojo.

As you look around the room you see different sizes of heavy bags, focus mitts, various weapons, wooden training dummies, and much more. The smell is a strange mixture of cedar, blood, and sweat. It is obvious that this place has been used for centuries to hone the mental skills of warriors, and now it belongs to you. Because it belongs to you, it can instantly be accessed by your mind. Any skill that you practice with your physical body can be trained here as well, in the mental dojo. Then you realize you are not alone here.

"Are you ready to begin?" You turn to see a figure in a dark cloak standing behind you. You cannot see a face, but you recognize the voice. It is the positive voice you created during the willpower exercise. The positive voice will be your guide and coach anytime you train in your mental training hall. He will push you when needed and make sure that your practice methods are perfect. Everything you accomplish in the mental dojo will carry over to your physical skills.

Now that you have established your mental dojo, you can expand further on your visualization training. Understand that the mental picture I presented here for your training area is simply my creation. Feel free to use it, or to create your own. Your mental training area can be anything you choose it to be, from a back alleyway in the inner city, to a sultry jungle military camp. The key is to vividly imagine it. You must actually feel the heat or cold, smell the sweat and blood, and experience the visualization like it is real. This will fire the neurons and muscles in your body to create actual physical response to your mental training.

Visualization Exercise Two
Perfecting Your Skills

Now we will use the power of visualization to help perfect your physical skills. This exercise can be used to train any technique you choose, but for the sake of this example, we will work on western boxing skills. Before we begin our training, find a quiet place where you won't be disturbed. Sit or lie down so that your physical body is comfortable, but make sure that you are not so comfortable that you will fall asleep. The goal is to be aware throughout the visualization practice and allow the mind and muscles to respond naturally to the training.

Breathe deeply and close your eyes. Imagine you are entering the doors of your mental dojo and you are prepared to train. Be sure to fully absorb the mental picture to the point that you actually feel the atmosphere of your training area. With the positive voice by your side to oversee your workout, you calmly wrap your hands and put on your bag gloves.

Imagine that you feel alive, quick on your feet, and powerful as you approach the heavy bag. See yourself throwing rapid boxing combinations that snap into the bag resulting in loud pops as they make contact. Visualize the bag folding from the power of your strikes. You can hear the chain that supports the heavy bag rattling violently after each hit. You glide around the bag with perfect footwork as you effortlessly fire your rapid combinations.

Pay attention to the details of every strike you throw during your visualization training. Notice how perfectly you execute each movement and the tremendous power that is transmitted into the heavy bag. See yourself ducking, bobbing, and weaving as you move around the bag and execute your strikes. Feel the sweat forming on your skin. It is happening in your mind, but it is real.

The positive inner voice taps you on the shoulder and draws your attention to a ring in the center of your mental dojo. Inside of the ring is a large muscular monster who is bouncing up and down and knocking his gloves together. He sneers at you through a mouthful of crooked teeth as he invites you to join him in the ring. As you duck under the ropes and climb into the ring, you feel great. Energy surges through your body as the bout begins.

The monster opponent lunges at you aggressively as he throws a lead punch followed by a cross. You slip the lead and parry away the cross before unleashing a lighting fast combination of blows to the head and body. Whenever the giant moves, you cut him off and counter punch with the same snapping power shots you had executed on the heavy bag. Soon the opponent can take no more and he falls. Allow the feeling of your perfect boxing strikes and evasion to sink in. Calm your heart, breathe deep, and slowly open your eyes to end the visualization exercise.

The key points of this exercise are first, to visualize yourself executing each technique with perfect precision and power, and second, to visualize those same techniques being effectively applied against an aggressive opponent. With this exercise, you can improve upon your physical skills at any time by using your mind's eye to visualize yourself executing your techniques flawlessly.

Visualization for Mental Preparation

Visualization exercises can also be used to mentally prepare yourself for upcoming challenges and improve your decision making in a real encounter. For example, say you are training for a future martial arts competition. Visualization exercises can give you self-confidence and improve your performance at the actual event. The benefits of these exercises can also be used beyond the martial arts, such as preparation for a public speaking event or a job interview. The following is an effective exercise that uses visualization for mental preparation.

Visualization Exercise Three
Mental Preparation

For the purposes of this exercise, you will prepare yourself for a potential mugging self-defense situation. Once again, find a quiet place to relax and perform the exercise. Close your eyes, breathe deep and imagine that you are walking home late at night in an unfamiliar neighborhood.

It is a chilly night, and the drizzle of rain has made the sidewalk and street glimmer with the reflection of the few streetlights that are working. As you walk, the frustration inside of you grows over the fact that your car has broken down and your cell phone battery is dead. If you can just find a convenience store, you will be able to call for a tow truck and a lift home.

Suddenly movement from across the street catches your eye. Two young men in their late teens or early twenties are walking a few hundred feet behind you. For no apparent reason they cross over to your side of the street and appear to pick up their pace. You begin to walk faster but they are closing the distance on you rapidly. Then one of them calls out, "Hey Buddy, you got any cigarettes?"

You turn to face the men and keep yourself in a slightly bladed position with your hands open at about chest level. You have not seen any weapons yet, but both individuals have their hands in their pockets. Your gut instinct is screaming that you're in trouble as you politely respond, "Sorry guys, I don't smoke." Their reply is the worst-case scenario you were hoping wouldn't happen, "How about you give us whatever you got in those pockets of yours then."

One of the men draws a small knife from his sweatshirt pocket and sticks it straight out towards your face. The second man begins to reach into your pockets to retrieve your belongings. What do you do? What decisions do you make when faced with this very dangerous scenario? Do you hand over your valuables, or do you try to outrun the robbers? How can you guarantee the men won't attack you even if you cooperate?

Maybe in this visualization exercise, you decide to cooperate. You hand over your wallet but at the same time, prepare to fight with everything you have should the robbers decide they want more than just your property. As you cooperate, you keep your hands up in a submissive position, but prepared to react if need be. You scan the area with your eyes to look for possible avenues of escape, environmental weapons, or potential witnesses to the incident. You also make a mental note of the physical description of your assailants.

If the visualization exercise you have chosen requires you to fight, vividly see yourself executing your self-defense techniques with perfection. Each strike you throw is lightning fast and impacts the intended target with extreme power. You are able to effortlessly evade attacks, defend, and counter strike. You are mentally prepared for anything the assailants throw at you.

By mentally rehearsing different scenarios in your visualization exercises, you will prepare your mind and be ready to react if a similar situation were to actually occur. Each time you perform the visualization exercise, you can vary the outcome, but one thing must remain constant. You always win. No matter what happens or how injured you become, you will survive. Always drill this fact into your visualization exercises.

As humans, we learn from our life experiences. If you were to survive an actual mugging, you would probably take steps to prevent that situation from occurring again. You would be more aware of your surroundings, not carry valuables, make sure your cell phone battery was charged, or maybe carry a weapon to defend yourself. The lessons learned from the actual mugging would be invaluable. Through your visualization exercises, you can prepare your mind in much the same way that an actual experience prepares you. Although visualization does not replace real world experiences, it does give you a valuable training tool to improve your skills.

Mind Clearing

In our fast-paced world, having a cluttered mind is a problem that many of us face on a daily basis. Random thoughts often cloud our head and distract us from our daily goals. In most cases, these random thoughts are merely bothersome obstacles in our ability to fully concentrate. For the martial artist however, having a cluttered mind in a life-or-death encounter can get you hurt or even killed.

Your mind is very similar to a river, constantly flowing with random ideas and thoughts. Just like some areas of a river might become stagnant and allow water to accumulate, your mind may allow random thoughts to pile up. We often see this happen in our day to day lives. While driving down the freeway, you might be thinking of what you are going to have for dinner, or the conversation you had earlier in the day with your boss.

Random thoughts can also interfere with our daily goals. It is quite common to begin a certain task only to get sidetracked and later ask yourself, "What was I doing?" For many people this can be a very serious problem that interferes with their home life and job performance. Thankfully, there are ways to slow down the flow of the river and clear out our minds.

As a young man I was fascinated with stories of the Samurai. I read many books about the exploits of famous swordsmen such as Takeda Shingen and Miyamoto Musashi. I was always amazed at how these ancient warriors could engage in battle with no fear or outside thoughts to distract them from their determination to win. It was during my studies of the Samurai that I first learned about the Japanese concept of *mushin no shin*, or mind with no mind.

During my decades of studying martial arts, I would encounter the concept of *mushin no shin* many times. Usually, it was referred to as simply *mushin*, or no mindedness. At a basic level it means to clear the mind of all thought, but on a much higher level it gives the practitioner the ability to be completely focused on the moment with no distractions. When the mind is clear, there is total awareness of the current situation with no outside thoughts to cause distraction or confusion.

Random thoughts manifest themselves in many different ways, from fear, revenge, anger, or the desire to achieve. The problem is that these manifestations in your head cause more harm than good. We become so engulfed in worrying about what might occur, or if we will fail and look bad to others, that we are sidetracked from the current task.

I remember watching an episode of the television series Kung-Fu from the 1970's, where the blind Master Po had the young boy Cain (Grasshopper) cross a narrow beam that was laying on the ground. The Master told Grasshopper to walk across the beam and not fall off, which he easily accomplished. Later, Master Po placed the beam across a pit of steaming liquid. He explained that the liquid was acid and again told Grasshopper to cross the beam.

With the acid pit below him, the boy became so afraid that he would fall, that he could not concentrate while crossing the beam. Halfway across, he loses his balance and falls into the pit of liquid. To his surprise, the liquid is only a pool of warm water and not really acid. Master Po points out to Grasshopper that he had walked the beam successfully numerous times when there was no danger. Only when his mind was filled with fear did he lose his concentration and fall.

The physical action of walking across the beam is the same regardless of whether it is flat on the ground, or over a pit of acid. Even if the beam was placed between the ledges of two skyscrapers, the physical action remains the same. What changes is our mental view of the action and our fear of the risk involved.

This fear usually manifests itself through our old enemy, the negative inner voice which tells us we will fail, injure ourselves, or die.

It is often wise to listen to what the negative inner voice tells us, because it might help steer us away from danger. In times of emergency such as a life-or-death encounter, we must be able to clear our mind of all thoughts, including the inner voice, so that we can focus on what must be done without hesitation or distraction. Many times, after we have dealt with a situation, we realize that the fear, apprehension, and anxiety leading up to the event was actually worse than the event itself.

The million-dollar question is, how do we clear our mind of the unwanted clutter and free ourselves from the distractions in our head? One way to accomplish this is to use the following exercise which I call, The White Board.

Mind Clearing Exercise One
The White Board

The White Board exercise is a simple but extremely effective method to immediately clear your mind of all unwanted thoughts. It can be done in as little as a few seconds with no preparation. First, recognize all of the random thoughts that are bouncing around inside of your head. Use your visualization skills to see the inside of your brain as a large white board similar to the ones used in a classroom or office to write down information.

All of your thoughts are on this white board in your brain. The board is so full of random thoughts and clutter that there is no room left to add any new thoughts. See this white board vividly in your mind's eye. You cannot have a thought without it appearing on the board. There is a silver tray below the board that holds an eraser. Pick up the eraser and in one or two broad sweeps, erase the white board.

All that is left is a shiny white surface where all of the random thoughts and clutter used to be. Your mind is instantly clear. No distractions, no outside thoughts. You have instantly erased them all. Your mind is now free to focus on the task at hand.

Once the white board is erased, it is important to keep the vision of a blank surface in your mind. New thoughts will quickly emerge and try to wiggle back into your brain. Simply keep the white board clear and don't let any new thoughts enter your mind and appear on the board. If thoughts do creep through, don't stress, or try to fight them off. You can pick the mental eraser up at any time and once again wipe the board clean if need be. After some practice with this exercise, you will literally be able to wipe your mind clean of unwanted thoughts in an instant, any time you wish. The following illustrations show the concept of the White Board exercise from a visual perspective.

The White Board Exercise

Step One- Close your eyes and recognize all of the random thoughts and clutter that currently fill your head. All of these thoughts distract you and make it extremely difficult for you to focus on the moment. Visualize your brain as a white board with these unwanted thoughts written across it. See the white board vividly in your mind's eye.

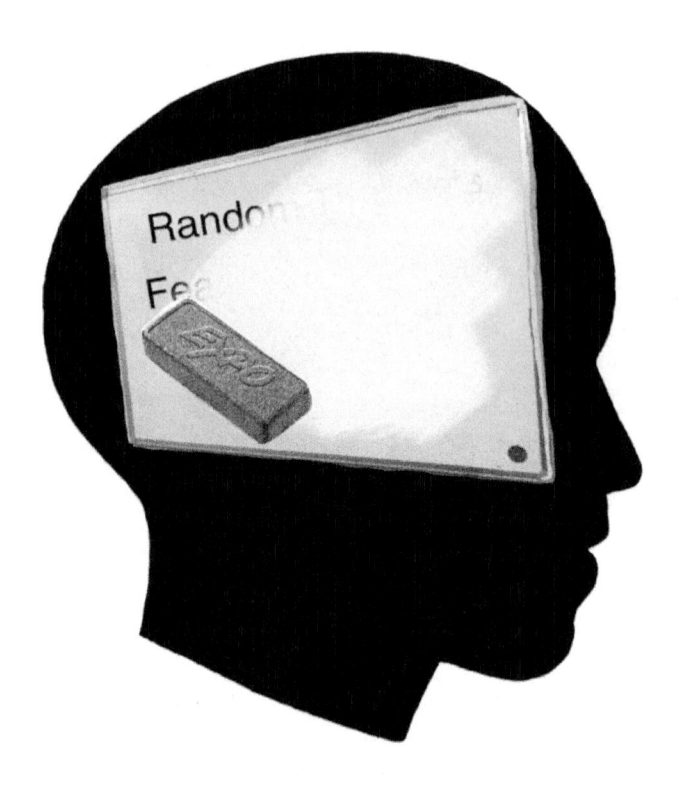

Step Two- When you are ready to clear your mind of all thoughts, wipe your mind clean by visualizing an eraser erasing the board in one or two broad strokes. The white board becomes blank, with nothing on it but the clear white surface. Keep the mind empty and clear by blocking any new thoughts from appearing on the white board. Don't become distracted by fighting off new thoughts however, if one appears, simply wipe it away in your mind's eye.

You can use the white board exercise to clear your mind instantly, right before a fight, before a public speaking event, or during an emergency where you need to have a clear mind to focus on the problem at hand. Once mastered, this exercise will serve you well.

Mind Clearing Exercise Two
The File Cabinet

Clearing the mind goes much deeper than simply removing unwanted thoughts from your head so you can focus clearly during combat. It can also be used to help you break the bonds of suppressed thoughts that have bothered you for years and continue to dwell deep inside of you.

We all have some unpleasant memories that dwell within our brain. They usually lie dormant but on occasion come to the surface and plague you with their presence. They might be memories of how you were embarrassed in front of your peers, or thoughts of how you were rejected or failed at something that was important to you. Whatever the incidents were that created the memories, they have a negative impact on your self-esteem. These memories might even be preventing you from taking chances in your life or making positive change.

The human mind is similar to a file cabinet. A memory of every event that has happened in your life is stored somewhere inside of that file cabinet in your head. Some of these files you use often and can access at will. Other files are tucked away inside of the cabinet drawer and can only be accessed when triggered by something. A perfect example of this is when you hear a song on the radio that instantly takes you back to an experience you had in in your life when that song was playing.

It is a fact that many people don't take chances in their lives because they are afraid of failure. They reflect back to a time when they failed at something and it felt awful. They don't want to experience that awful feeling again. Many people are afraid they will look bad to their peers or family, so they never try anything new if there is a risk of failure involved. We see this often in the martial arts where a person who achieves a black belt in one system refuses to learn a new style because they don't want to put on a white belt again and risk failure. They like being the black belt and don't want to be seen as a novice.

To perform the exercise, close your eyes and visualize the file cabinet in your head where all of your memories both good and bad are stored. See the huge file cabinet vividly in your mind's eye. With hundreds of drawers, it fills an entire room. Every memory you have is stored somewhere in these drawers. Many of the memories are trivial or you have forgotten they even exist. After a brief search, you open one of the drawers and retrieve a file. This file contains the unwanted memory that clutters your brain and prevents you from achieving your goals. Next to the giant file cabinet is a paper shredder. Take the unwanted memory file and feed it into the shredder. As the shredder grinds the file into tiny paper shreds, you realize that you are finally free of this painful memory and it will no longer bother you. Closed the mental file cabinet and open your eyes.

The key point to this exercise is that ultimately you control the file cabinet inside of your head. You are the one that can rearrange the files or even remove files if you choose to do so. The file cabinet exercise gives you the power to get rid of memories that are obstructing your growth and preventing you from improving as a martial artist and a person. It is important to mention that in order to get better, we must learn from our mistakes. When you use this exercise, get rid of the memory that stifles you and prevents you from taking risks, but don't forget the important lesson you learned from that memory.

Breathing

Proper breathing is absolutely critical for fighting and self-defense, but it is often overlooked by martial artists. When breathing is overlooked, you will tire quickly, lose focus, lack power, become lightheaded, and have a greater risk of injury from your attacker. By fully understanding the proper way to breath during combat, and incorporating a few simple breathing exercises into your training, you will gain great benefits that will help you in fighting and in other areas of your life.

When you are involved in a self-defense situation or a violent encounter, your body will immediately go into fight or flight mode. Your heart will start beating rapidly, Adrenaline will surge through your body, and your breathing will become much faster than normal. All of these natural occurrences will cause you to lose your fine motor skills. Tunnel vision will occur and your ability to focus on the larger picture will be greatly diminished. In many cases, this can cause a person to freeze and be unable to react to the threat. By Controlling your breathing, you can stay focused and reduce the impact of these effects.

Guidelines for Proper Breathing

Don't hold your breath

There are some general guidelines associated with proper breathing that can easily be adapted. The first is to avoid holding your breath. This is a very common mistake that martial artists make when fighting. They take a large breath and hold it as they strike or defend. Then they release the air and immediately take another breath and hold it as they attack or defend again. Within seconds, they are exhausted.

Once you become winded in a fight, you lose about eighty percent of your skill level. Your movements will become slow, telegraphed, and lack power. When this occurs, you become a sitting duck for the attacker to pick off at will. You must pay close attention to your breathing when training and sparring. Make sure that you are breathing in a steady pattern as you move, and never holding your breath.

Exhale when you strike and defend

Always exhale when you strike the opponent or defend against an attack. This will add power to your blows and prevent you from being injured easily from an opponent's strike. You can test this guideline yourself by striking a heavy bag. First, throw a few strikes on the bag as you breathe in, then execute a few additional strikes while exhaling as you throw each blow. You will immediately feel the difference between the two sets of strikes. The blows that are thrown while exhaling will have much more power.

Exhaling forcefully as you get hit by the opponent can help you absorb an attack and prevent possible injury to your internal organs. When you breathe out forcefully, your stomach muscles tighten, and your body becomes more prepared for the impact of an opponent's strike. When you are relaxed or caught off guard, the same strike can cause you much more damage.

The simplest method of breathing when striking or receiving a blow from the opponent is to exhale forcefully through your mouth with a sound similar to, "hwoot". You must learn to do this while keeping your teeth clinched together and not opening your mouth wide. If you take a punch to the jaw while your mouth is open, you risk having your jaw broken. Practice exhaling when you spar or strike the heavy bag by keeping the teeth clinched and slightly opening your lips while you make the "hwoot" sound every time you hit.

Breathe in through the nose and out through the mouth

During a violent encounter, you will experience severe stress and possibly start to hyperventilate. It is vital to control your breathing and slow your heart rate. By breathing in through your nose and out through the mouth, you can calm yourself, slow your heart rate, and better focus on the situation. Don't force your breathing, just allow it to happen naturally. Fill the lungs from the bottom and relax the diaphragm to expel the air.

For some people, breathing through the nose might be difficult. I have a difficult time breathing through my nose because of a deviated septum I received from years of boxing. If this is the case, it is ok to breath in through the mouth, just keep the teeth lightly clinched and open the lips slightly to bring the air in.

Use a spirit yell

Warriors have used a battle cry or spirit yell since the beginning of time when humans first engaged in warfare. Examples of those who have been known for their battle cries throughout the ages include the Roman gladiators, Native American warriors, the Vikings, and the famous rebel yell of Confederate soldiers during the Civil War.

Yelling or screaming during combat is a natural phenomenon that is not unique to humans. From a lion's roar to the screeching of monkeys during fighting, battle cries are very common throughout the animal kingdom to intimidate and startle an adversary.

The primary purpose of a spirit yell is to ignite courage and killer instinct within you as you launch your attack. It is also very effective for striking fear into your enemies. The spirit yell also provides protection from attack by tightening the muscles in your body to prepare for a possible counterattack. A spirit yell should be used sparingly and saved for those situations where you need to generate extreme power or deliver a coup de grace attack to finish your attacker.

Although many martial arts employ some form of a battle cry, the traditional Japanese arts have taken it to a high level with the use of a technique known as a kiai. The use of the kiai is often found in the traditional kata or forms when executing power strikes. The Japanese battle cry, "Banzai", was also made famous by the Kamikaze suicide bombers during World War II.

To execute a spirit yell, tighten your stomach muscles, and exhale forcefully as you shout. There are many types of sounds that can be made as you shout such as, "Yaaaa", "Ooose", or the traditional, "Hiyaaah"! The sound really doesn't matter as long as your spirit yell is short. Loud, and powerful.

I recommend that you start incorporating the spirit yell into your daily training. Use it when sparring or striking the heavy bag. One great exercise is to set an egg timer for three minutes as you strike the heavy bag, a makiwara board, or focus mitts with a partner. The instant the timer rings, make a final strike to the target with a powerful spirit yell. You will instantly feel the difference in the power of your strikes when a battle cry is employed.

Breathing exercises

During my years of martial arts training, I have learned literally hundreds of breathing exercises that range from simple natural breathing to complicated breathing patterns and reverse breathing methods. I personally believe that the three breathing exercises we will discuss below are the best of them all. These are the only breathing exercises I have used for close to thirty years.

You might ask yourself why you should practice breathing exercises at all. Are they really needed? The fact is that breathing exercises will provide a tremendous amount of benefit to not only your martial arts training, but also your daily life. Just some of the benefits that daily breathing exercises can provide include, relaxation, reduced stress, lower heart rate, clearer focus, and more energy. Let's take a look at what I believe are the three best breathing exercises you can perform.

Breathing Exercise One
Heaven's Breath

The Heaven's Breath exercise is my go-to breathing exercise that I use when I need to focus, catch my breath, reduce stress, and slow my heart rate. I use it daily for the many health benefits it provides. It can be performed anywhere in less than a minute.

I first learned this breathing exercise while studying the martial art of Aikido. We would perform it at the end of our class to calm the mind and gather our energy. I have never found a breathing exercise that is better. Let's get started.

Begin with the feet shoulder's width apart and the hands held at about waist level with the palms facing inward as if holding a ball. Relax your entire body and round the shoulder blades. Lightly place the tip of your tongue against the roof of your mouth just behind your upper teeth. Breathe deep and naturally, in through the nose and out through the mouth. Begin to slowly raise your arms upward Infront of your body as you inhale and completely fill your lungs with air.

As you fill your lungs with air, continue to raise your arms upward above your head until they point straight up to the sky. Your eyes follow the motion of your arms as they travel upward. Complete your inhalation as the hands reach their upward position above your head. The palms are still facing inward just slightly wider than shoulders width.

Turn the palms outward and slowly start to lower your arms down to the sides as you begin to exhale. Your eyes follow the decent of your arms. The body remains relaxed and there is no tension as the arms are lowered. Your breath and the arms move in harmony with one another.

The arms continue to lower to your sides as you exhale. Both arms travel down and cross in front of your abdomen as you complete your exhalation. The below photographs show this action as the arms come down and cross.

You will now start to inhale again as you slowly separate your hands outwards with the palms facing inwards. Your eyes focus down in front of your body.

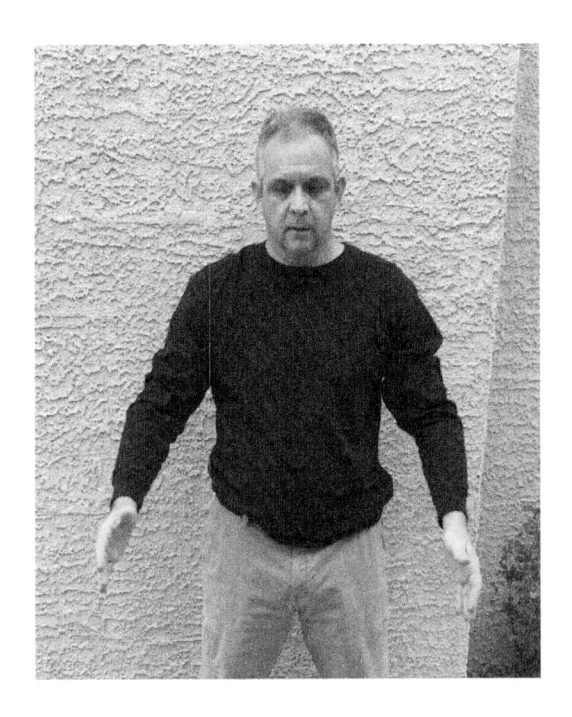

Complete your second inhalation as the arms come to rest at your sides with the palms facing forward towards the front. Start to exhale for the second time as you bring your hands back towards the center of your body. As your hands come to rest back in their original starting position, complete your exhalation.

Hold this final position for a few seconds and imagine energy surging between the palms of your hands, then repeat the entire exercise again. After completing three repetitions of the Heaven's Breath exercise, breathe naturally and completely relax. Clear your mind of all thoughts as you hold this position for about thirty seconds. It is very common to feel a tingling sensation in the hands and fingers at this point. Your hands may also feel warm.

After you have completed the Heaven's Breath exercise, you will feel calm, stress free, and much more focused. This makes the exercise an extremely effective tool to use when you have just experienced a traumatic event such as a car accident, or a violent encounter. It can also be highly beneficial to use this exercise to calm yourself prior to events such as public speaking or a job interview. I do the Heaven's Breath exercise in the morning to start my day, and just prior to bed at night. I truly believe this is the best breathing exercise a person can do.

Breathing Exercise Two
The Dynamite Box

The Dynamite Box is a breathing exercise that is used to gather your energy and prepare your mind and body for action. It gets its name from the motion your arms make during the exercise which resembles the motions used to detonate dynamite with one of the old dynamite boxes that miners used.

A Dynamite Box

The Dynamite Box differs from the Heaven's Breath exercise in that it is used more to energize you rather than to calm and relax the mind and body. Your breathing and the movement of your arms are done at a faster pace than they were while performing the

Heaven's Breath exercise. In the following photographs we will break down each motion of the exercise in detail.

Start by standing with your feet shoulders width apart, knees slightly bent, and your arms held at your sides with the palms facing forward. Your back is straight, and the shoulders are slightly curved. Relax the shoulders and breathe naturally.

Raise your hands upward from the side as you start to inhale deeply. Your eyes stay focused forward as you visualize yourself gathering energy around you with the arms as they rise.

As your arms rise up and your hands come above the shoulders, start to bring them closer together and bend the arms. The hands end up coming together at about forehead level in front of your face. You then push downward with the hands in front of your body. This motion is exactly like the motion you would use to detonate the dynamite. Your hands come to rest in front of your lower stomach with one palm over the other to complete the exercise. As you perform this exercise, imagine you are collecting energy from the air all around you, bringing it into your body at your head and then pushing it down to your lower abdomen. Just like charging a battery, your body is filled with this energy that gives you the power and endurance needed to accomplish your goals.

Forging The Mind And Body

It is important to note the differences between the Heaven's

Breath and the Dynamite box exercise. Although they both can be used to clear your mind, and relax the body, the Heaven's Breath exercise is designed to eliminate stress, slow your heart rate, and catch your breath. The Dynamite Box is designed to energize you, get your blood flowing and prepare you for action.

We will now look at another breathing exercise that can be incorporated with the two previous exercises. I call it the Table Top.

Breathing Exercise Three
The Table Top

The Table Top Is a medium paced breathing exercise that gets the blood flowing through your arms, loosens up the back and spine, energizes the body, and can be used to prepare you for the possible impact from a blow. Unlike the previous two exercises which required you to relax, this exercise requires you to tense slightly and feel some resistance in your arms and body as you move.

Start with your hands about ten inches in front of your stomach with your palms facing the ground. Breathe in through your nose and start to fill your lungs from the bottom to the top with air. As you inhale, move your hands forward slightly and then out to the sides. The movement of your arms resembles the action you would use to brush across a flat table top with your hands.

As the arms move outward, tighten your muscles slightly and feel a slight resistance as if you were moving your arms under water. The hands continue to move out to your sides as you fill your lungs with air. When they reach a point of almost full exstention, start to circle them back towards your hips as if you were a gun fighter preparing to draw your pistols. You complete your inhalation as the hands finish their circle near your hips.

Next you will start to exhale as you push your hands forward across the imaginary table top. Again, you should imagine some resistance and tense your body slightly as you push forward. You will complete your exhalation just as the hands reach almost full exstension. You then separate your hands and start to inhale to repeat the exercise. The entire motion of your arms during inhalation and exhalation will make a horizontal circular motion in front of your body. Repeat this exercise three times, then lower your arms to your side and relax. The below photographs show the series of movements for this exercise.

Forging The Mind And Body

On the surface the three breathing exercises shown above might appear quite similar, however they each have a different tempo, feel, and ultimate purpose. The Heaven's Breath exercise calms the mind, reduces stress, and relaxes the body. The Dynamite Box exercise generates energy, stabalizes your posture, and helps to focus the mind. The Table Top exercise generates power, builds strength, and prepares the body for attack. When used together, the three exercises constitute a dynamic breathing system that can improve your martial arts skills and benefit your health and life.

There is one more breathing exercise we will cover in this chapter that is very effective for reducing stress, alleviating pain, and helping you feel better when you are sick. It is called The Sustained Throat Growl.

Breathing Exercise Four
The Sustained Throat Growl

Moaning is a natural human reaction when sick, injured, or suffering. It creates a soothing effect on the mind and body that can alleviating discomfort. In many cases, the vibrations created by moaning are relaxing and can help us cope with pain. The Sustained Throat Growl exercise is a simple breathing tool that utilizes this concept. There is no movement involved in this exercise so It can be performed from any position you choose. The only requirement will be that you make a little noise.

To begin, find a quiet place to sit or lie down. Close your eyes and place your tongue gently on the roof of your mouth just behind your upper teeth. Take a deep breath in and completely fill up your lungs with air, starting from the bottom. As you start to exhale, keep the mouth closed, but open your throat and the back of your nasal passage. You will use your voice box to make a low level hum the entire time that you exhale. This hum comes from just below the voice box and is similar to a low growl that an animal might make when it's warning you to stay back.

The noise that accompanies this sustained growl is similar to an, "Uuuuughhhhh". The sound and growl in conjunction with the hollowing of your throat and nasal passage will create a low level vibration that you can feel in your mouth and throat. By placing the tip of the tongue on the roof of your mouth, the vibration will carry over to your head as well. You will sustain this growl for the entire time your exhale. Your exhale should be very slow and long until there is no more air left in your lungs. This is very similar to a cat purring.

The growl originates in the same spot that you feel in your neck when you clear your throat. Three actions occuring simultaniously create the vibration. These actions are the exhalation, the hum or moaning type noise, and the growl. When done correctly, you will immediately feel the vibration in your head and neck.

The longer you can exhale during this exercise, the better. Over time you should strive to increase the length of your exhalation and allow the vibration to be felt below the head and neck, and into the upper body as well. Once you have completed an exhalation, take a normal inhalation, breath normal for a few cycles, and then take a large breath and repeat the exercise again. You may repeat this exercise as many times as needed to assist with alleviating pain and discomfort.

The Sustained Growl Exercise

Explosive Power

Having the ability to instantly launch an explosive attack from stillness is an extremely powerful skill to possess. When most martial artists hear the word explosive they think of power and speed, but power and speed are not necessarily explosive in nature. We have all seen examples of people who are goliaths with extreme strength, or someone with extremely fast hands, but in many cases these individuals lack explosiveness in their strikes. In this chapter we will look at ways to develop explosiveness and incorporate it into your techniques.

To start, lets define exactly what we mean when we use the term explosive power. Explosive power is the ability to go from zero to one hundred in a fraction of a second. Similar to pulling the trigger on a gun. When properly applied, the opponent will be hit with a combination of speed and power before he realizes what has occurred. He won't even know what hit him.

To differentiate between normal speed and power and explosive power, think of the following examples. In the first example, you are training on the heavy bag. You are moving around the bag with fluid footwork, bobbing and weaving as you throw rapid strikes. Your movements are crisp and thrown with excellent speed and power, but they are not explosive.

In the second example, you are standing completely still as you face the heavy bag. Your arms are up with your hands held in a non-threatening manner at about chest level. Suddenly, you explode with a hook punch that cracks into the heavy bag, folding it in the middle as it hits. If someone were watching you, they might have missed it because it happened so fast. This is explosive power. Now let's look at the components that make up explosive power.

The Components of Explosive Power

Just like an explosive device needs various components such as powder, a detonator, or a fuse to properly function, explosive power requires the combination of several components to be effective. Some of these components may seem like common sense at first but remember that it is the combination of these components that will create the ability to powerfully explode with an attack.

Start from stillness

One of the keys to explosive power is the ability to move instantly, straight to the target from any stationary position. To do this, you must be able to generate power through proper body mechanics without winding up or pulling back to execute a strike. When a violent encounter begins, you will often be caught off guard and standing still. If a situation is escalating and you assume an aggressive posture or begin moving around like a boxer, the adversary will expect you to attack, and he won't be caught off guard. By starting from stillness, you can gain the advantage of surprise.

In the below series of photos, a confrontation begins between the attacker in white and the defender who is in black. The defender is standing in a non-aggressive posture with his hands up. As the attacker begins to shove the defender, he instantly explodes with simultaneous shoulder strikes that snap him around and into a rear naked choke. This entire technique takes place in a split second and is executed in an explosive manner. The attacker ends up in the choke hold before he realizes what has occurred.

You can practice this component of explosive power by standing still in front of a heavy bag or some other type of striking target. Begin with your hands either at your sides, or up at chest level. Remain totally relaxed and instantly explode with a strike to the target. Don't worry about generating a lot of power at this point, but rather exploding instantly from a stationary position.

Example of Explosive Power-Shoulder Snap to Rear Naked Choke

From a stationary position, the defender explodes instantly with a shoulder snap that spins the opponent into a rear naked choke hold. The shoulder snap is done by striking the opponent's rear shoulder back while simultaniously striking his lead shoulder inward. When the two shoulder strikes are combined, the oppoent is instantly spun counter clockwise. As he spins, he automatically winds up in the rear naked choke hold. This movement is highly effective, but must be done with explosive power in order to work.

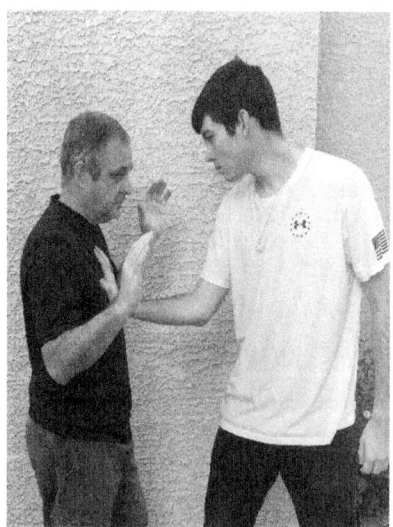

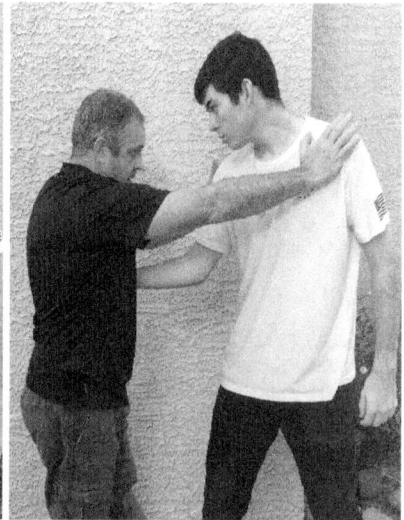

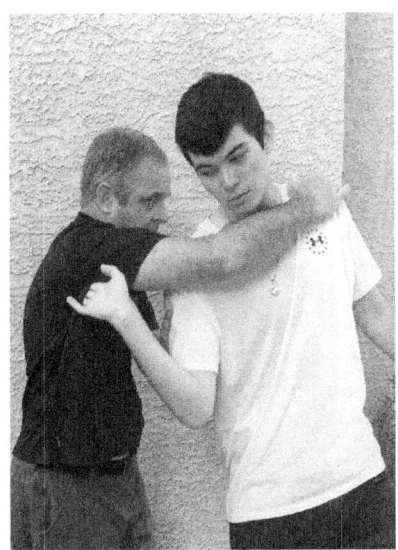

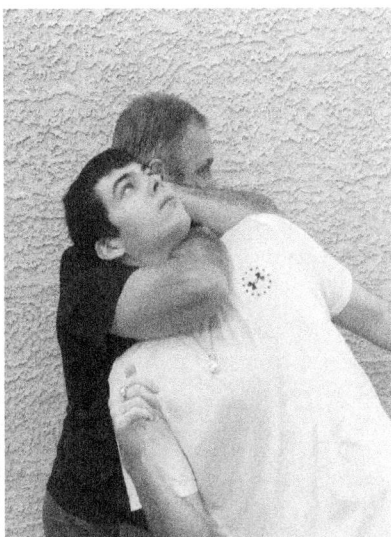

Explode from any position

Not only is it vital to be able to explode from complete stillness, but you must also be able to explode from any position you happen to be in. For example, you might be kneeling, sitting, or leaning against a countertop when the violent encounter occurs. You normally won't have time to reposition yourself for an attack. If you do have time and change positions before you attack, the opponent will be more prepared for any action you take.

Explode from any Point

Exploding from any point means that you attack from wherever your attacking limb might be. If you extend your arm to block the opponent's attack, you explode with your strike from the point where your defending arm contacted his attacking limb. In the below photos, the attacker throws a lead punch which the defender parries with a wing arm deflection. From the point of the deflection, the defender explodes directly into the attacker with an elbow strike. There is no retraction of his arm or wasted movement. In fact, a person observing the encounter would believe that there was only one single movement on the part of the defender. It should also be noted that the defender grabs the attacker's wrist and pulls him into the elbow which adds to the explosive power of the attack.

Do not telegraph your movements or intentions
When you launch your attack, it must happen instantly with no indicators that it is going to occur. Your striking weapon explodes straight to the target without cocking back the limb, shifting position, or moving your body in any way. Even looking at the target you intend to strike will telegraph your attack. The instant that you telegraph your intentions, the attack loses its explosive power.

The trigger concept
The trigger is a mental concept used to instantly launch your attack. Think of it as the button on the detonator of your explosives or the trigger on a gun. You will be perfectly still and relaxed, and when the button is pushed, or the trigger is pulled, you will explode into your attack with total commitment. Later we will discuss an exercise to fully develop the trigger concept.

Penetration and follow through
Always strike through the target and penetrate completely when attacking. This is an extremely important component of explosive power. In the interest of safety, it is common to pull punches or practice with light contact when training with a partner. This must always be avoided when developing explosive power. Because you have to explode completely through the target with total commitment, it is best to train with equipment like focus mitts or a heavy bag.

Snap and recovery
In addition to penetration and follow through, snap and recovery are also vital components. Your strike must snap back with the same speed that it was launched as you recover to a defensive

position. The snap back generates increased power that is similar to the crack of a whip. To grasp this concept fully, think of trying to break a board that someone is hold up with one hand. If your strike lacks snap, the board will be knocked out of the persons hand but will not break. The only way you can break a board held in this manner is with snap. You can also tell if a strike has proper snap when you hit a heavy bag because the bag will bend in the center and move very little rather than swing back due to power alone. A strike with snap will also make a cracking sound when you hit the bag instead of a solid thud that a shot makes when delivered with power alone.

Relaxation

Relaxation is critical to explosive power. If you have tension in your body prior to your attack, it will slow you down and limit your ability to launch your strike. Again, think of a nuclear explosion that happens instantly from the completely relaxed state of splitting an atom. However, relaxation is not being a limp noodle or being unprepared. Relaxation is a state of preparedness like the calm before the storm or a cat on the prowl.

Proper body alignment and mechanics

Another element to ensure maximum explosive power is proper body alignment. To transfer power into the target requires the knees, legs, hips, shoulders, elbows, and arms to all work in conjunction. If any of these links in the chain are out of alignment, maximum power will not be transferred to the target.

Use the ground

Just like a runner uses the starting blocks to propel themselves forward when the pistol fires, you should use the ground as a base to propel yourself into your strikes. The classic example of using the ground to generate power is the action you take when pushing a stalled car out of the street. If you were to stand up straight and not use the ground to push from, you would have a very difficult time moving the car.

Total commitment

Total commitment is a vital component for explosive power. Once you decide to launch your attack, there should be no hesitation and no second thought. I will once again use the analogy of bomb exploding. Once the decision is made to push the button on the detonator, there is no turning back. This is also where other factors we have discussed come into play such as will power and mindset.

Explosive Power Exercise One
The Trigger

The purpose of this exercise is to create a mental trigger that will instantly launch you into action when activated. Stand in front of a striking target or a heavy bag at a distance where you could reach out and touch the target without stepping forward. You should be completely still and relaxed, with your hands at your sides, and knees slightly bent.

For this exercise we will use the trigger word, "Bam", but you could choose any word you want for your trigger word. The word itself is irrelevant. When you say the word "bam" in your head, you will instantly strike the bag with a straight punch directly from your side. At this point, we are not concerned with extreme power in the strike. The goal is to develop a mental trigger that ignites your attack instantly.

Every time you mentally recite the word "bam", you will

explode directly into the target with your punch, using your entire body. The feeling should be like a giant muscle twitch that engulfs you for a split second when you strike. Your strike should be hitting the target before you are finished saying the trigger word in your head.

You can take this exercise a step further by starting from different positions, such as standing sideways with the bag, or with your hands up at waist or chest level. Regardless of where you begin, you must start totally relaxed and explode with your entire body when the trigger word is recited in your head.

Again, the feeling you should get in your body when you pull the mental trigger, is an instant twitch of all your muscles. The feeling should seem similar to how your body reacts when you touch the surface of a hot stove or when you are accidently shocked by an electrical wire. A sudden forward jolt of energy as you explode.

Explosive Power Exercise Two
Combining the Components

Once you have developed your mental trigger and have the ability to go from zero to one hundred in an instant, it is time to start combining all of the components of explosive power into your strikes. This step in the process will not be easy, and will take a lot of work, but the results will be well worth it. It is beneficial to have a training partner assist you to ensure you are properly utilizing all of the components when you strike.

Start the same as you did in the trigger exercise, facing your striking target in a relaxed position with your knees bent slightly. You should be able to reach out and touch your intended target.

As you say your mental trigger word, all of the components for explosive power must happen simultaneously.

As your strike is launched, it travels from the point or position it is in, directly to the target with no wind up or telegraphing of the attack. Your knees should feel as though they collapse for a split instant and then spring you forward, similar to compressing a spring and then releasing it. Your feet push from the ground to generate power which travels up your leg, into the waist and hips, up the back and shoulders, and through the arm to the target. Your hips rotate with a snap as the strike travels forward.

Your strike travels through the target and then immediately snaps back with full commitment and no hesitation. You will know when all of the components have been combined correctly by the loud crack when your strike impacts the target. The target will bend in the middle and jolt aggressively without swinging or moving back.

Although you can practice this exercise on any target, and even in the air, the best target to use is a heavy bag. The heavy bag will resemble striking a human body and will provide you with the most feedback on your strike based on how it moves when hit. The below illustrations show this exercise being performed.

It is also important to note that as the lead foot steps forward, your strike makes contact just before the foot touches down on the ground. In some cases, the foot will land with a loud stomp. This directs your body weight and power into the target rather than into the ground.

Forging The Mind And Body

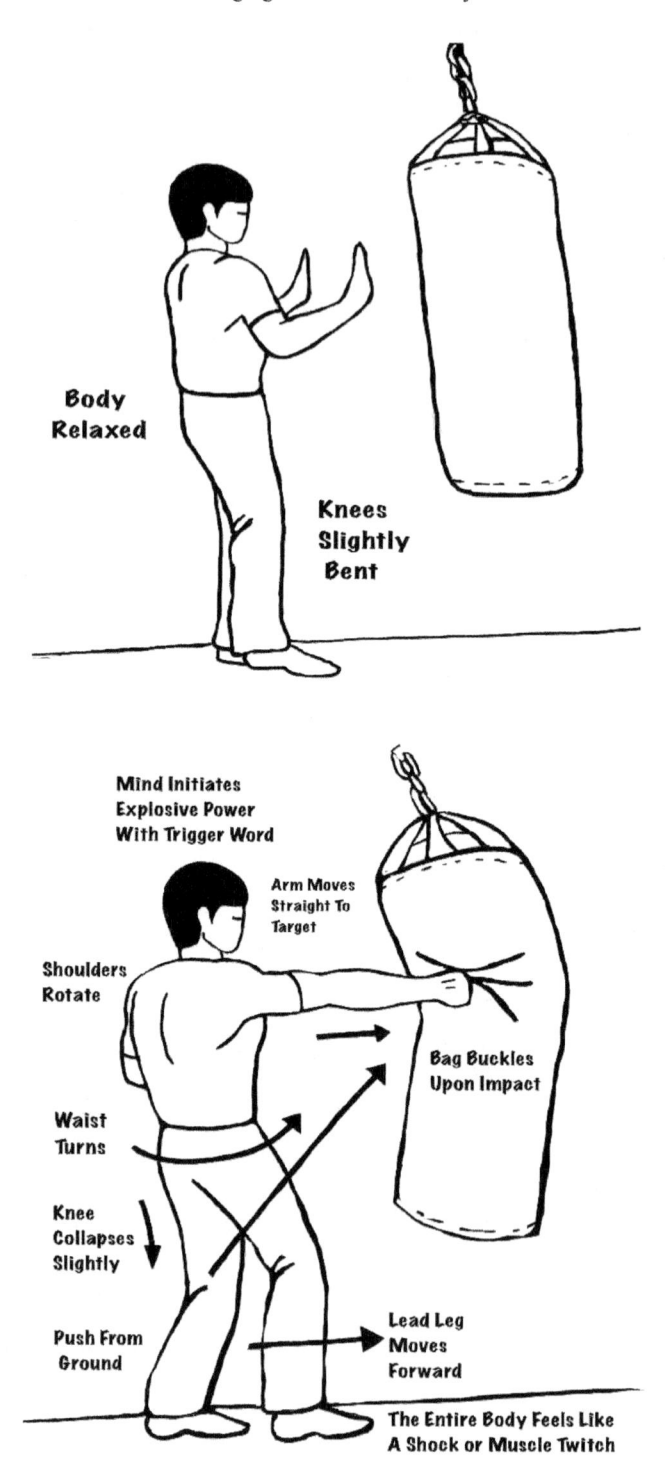

Body Relaxed

Knees Slightly Bent

Mind Initiates Explosive Power With Trigger Word

Arm Moves Straight To Target

Shoulders Rotate

Bag Buckles Upon Impact

Waist Turns

Knee Collapses Slightly

Push From Ground

Lead Leg Moves Forward

The Entire Body Feels Like A Shock or Muscle Twitch

Explosive Power Exercise Three
Energy Packing

The energy packing exercise is a very effective visualization technique that will help you build your explosive power. One of the benefits of this exercise is that it can be done anywhere and at any time.

Begin with by standing completely relaxed with your hands at your sides. Breath in deep through your nose and imagine a bright yellow energy entering your body through the top of your head. This energy is a powerful electric energy similar to a lightning bolt. Visualize the energy traveling from the crown of your head down your neck along your spine. When it reaches your lower abdomen, it begins to swirl into a sphere. You feel it getting warm in your belly as it starts to spin faster.

Now you will visualize grabbing the swirling sphere of energy and squeezing it into a smaller ball. Every time you squeeze it, it becomes smaller and tighter in your lower abdomen. This is similar to squeezing a rubber ball except instead of a normal ball, it is a ball of pure energy. The tighter you pack the energy ball; the more pressure builds.

Once the sphere of energy has been packed tightly into the size of a dime, the pressure is immense and ready to explode outward. When your trigger word is said in your mind, the energy will suddenly be released and explode from your abdomen, out through your arms and into your strike.

After a little practice, you will be able to create the compressed ball of energy in your abdomen almost instantly. You can trigger the release of the energy instantly when you strike with explosive power. When you have become proficient with this exercise, incorporate it into the previous exercise of combining all of the components of explosive energy.

As we close out the chapter on explosive power, keep in mind that the ultimate goal is to provide you with the ability to instantly explode at any time and from any position with maximum power. This requires not only the proper unification of all of the components we have discussed above, but also the proper mental components as well. Don't make the mistake of dismissing the information and exercises contained here as esoteric or not realistic. Also don't make the mistake of thinking you can acquire explosive power without the physical work. If you take the time to fully develop this skill, it will be a valuable element of your fighting system.

Adapt and Flow

One of the golden rules in life is that nothing ever goes as planned. Having the ability to adapt and go with the flow are critical skills to have when things don't go as expected in a violent encounter. In this chapter we will look at various methods that will enhance your ability to adapt to the unknown and flow with anything your opponent might throw your way.

The first key to adaptability is not relying too much on one technique or version of a technique. While the old saying is true that it is better to master one technique than to be familiar with a thousand techniques, if your opponent knows how to counter the one skill you have mastered, you will have problems. This doesn't mean that you have to master hundreds of techniques to be an effective fighter, but what it does mean is that you must be able to adapt and flow between a few solid techniques to address any situation.

Imagine that you are going to fight an opponent in the ring who is well known for his powerful cross kick. You have watched several videos of his previous fights to prepare for the match. In every video you have seen, he destroys his opponent's legs with that fierce kick. You focus your training specifically to defend against the cross kick by lifting your lead leg, and countering with a rear punch.

On the day of the fight, the bell rings and you advance towards your opponent. He immediately throws a cross kick which you lift your leg to avoid, but before you can launch your counterattack, the opponent flows from the missed cross kick into a round kick. The kick impacts your support leg and knocks you to the ground. Every time you try to counter the opponent's cross kick, he instantly flows into another attack. When the fight is over, your opponent is the victor.

In the above scenario, the opponent was able to take his signature technique and adapt it to various situations. A mistake that many martial artists make is practicing a technique for one specific situation and not learning how to adapt it to other possible scenarios. Just like a video game creator must think of every possible action a player can make and program a response into the game, you should also train each technique with the consideration of all possible outcomes. The follow exercise is very beneficial for practicing this skill.

Adapt and Flow Exercise One
What If

Most martial arts instructors hate it when they are teaching a class and they get the infamous "What if?" questions from their students. It never fails, you are demonstrating a technique and one of your students responds with, "But what if the guy hits you with his other hand?" "What if he has a knife?" The "what if" questions can keep coming and coming.

In my early days I used to hate these questions and it was common for me to respond to students that you can "what if" everything to death, but this is how you execute the technique". Then I realized that the "what if" questions are actually vital to consider and should be incorporated into your training.

In this exercise, you will pair off with a training partner and choose a specific technique to work on. It can be a simple lead punch, a defensive movement, or a more complicated grappling technique. Begin by simply practicing the technique over and over again until you are very proficient in executing it in its basic form. Once you have reached a level of proficiency in the basic technique, have your training partner start the "what if" process.

If you are practicing a simple lead punch for example, your

training partner will provide you with "what if" scenarios that you must respond to. He may parry your punch with his hand, roll back to avoid the attack, sidestep offline, or try to jam the attack before it gets started. In the beginning stages, your partner should start off slow and verbalize his intent. He can say, "What if I duck under the punch, or block with my arm?" You must decide how you will respond to his actions.

It is important to think about every possible scenario you can imagine and try to incorporate them into the exercise. After a while, your training partner will speed up his "what if" responses and stop verbalizing them to you. You will find that there are actually a lot less "what if" scenarios than what you might have initially imagined.

After you get to the point where you are successful in reacting to whatever situation your opponent gives you, switch to a new technique and start the entire process over again. Stay focused on the goal which is to become proficient at adapting to any situation you might encounter. Again, start slowly with verbal cues and gradually build up to full speed with random reactions and no verbal cues. You will find that the skill you develop from this exercise will be extremely valuable.

One area where this exercise is vital is joint manipulation. When you apply a wrist lock or an arm bar on your training partner and he resists to escape, you must be able to adapt in order to maintain the lock or flow with his movement into another lock or attack. The only way to develop this skill and make your joint locks effective in a real situation is with a training partner who resists.

Flow and reaction

I believe that flow and reaction are brother and sister skills in the martial arts. One compliments the other and having good flow will increase your reaction skills tremendously. Being able to react quickly to an opponent's attack will also allow you to flow faster into a counterattack. Before we discuss ways to improve our flow and reaction time, let's make sure we understand what each of these attributes actually are.

Flow is the ability to transition from one technique or body position to another in a seamless manner without hesitation or interruption of movement. Similar to how water rushes down a mountain stream, flowing around rocks or other obstructions without a break in motion.

Reaction is your ability to identify a threat or situation and immediately respond to it. A perfect analogy is the combat soldier who suddenly sees a grenade land in his bunker and immediately picks it up and throws it back at the enemy a split second before it explodes. The soldier reacts instantly to the threat with no hesitation or second thought.

An example of flow and reaction combined into one fluid motion would be as follows. You throw a lead punch to the opponent's head which he parries inward with an open hand on your wrist. You react to the force of his parry and flow directly into a round elbow strike. The entire movement happens in one fluid motion.

I first began learning the concept of flow while studying the Filipino martial arts in the early nineties. During that time, we practiced numerous flow drills that consisted of either shadow boxing known as Carenza, or attack and counter flows from the twelve angles of attack. Although these drills were very effective for developing flow and reaction skills, I later learned a variation of the twelve angles drill that proved extremely effective.

In 2004, I started studying the Batangas System of Arnis under Guro Dan Cepeda. I immediately noticed a difference in how the twelve angles drills were done compared to what I had previously studied. For one, Guro Cepeda would randomly strike the angles at almost full force. He would also strike the angles quickly with little time to counterattack between each strike. This method really jumpstarted my own flow and reaction skills in a very short period of time.

Adapt and Flow Exercise Two
Twelve Angles of Attack (Fluid)

For this exercise you will learn the twelve angles of attack from the Batangas Arnis System. You will then practice these angles in a fluid manner by flowing from one attack to the next without interruption of motion. Once you are familiar with the angles in sequence, you will randomly strike all of the angles in a fluid manner. Let's take a detailed look at the twelve angles of attack.

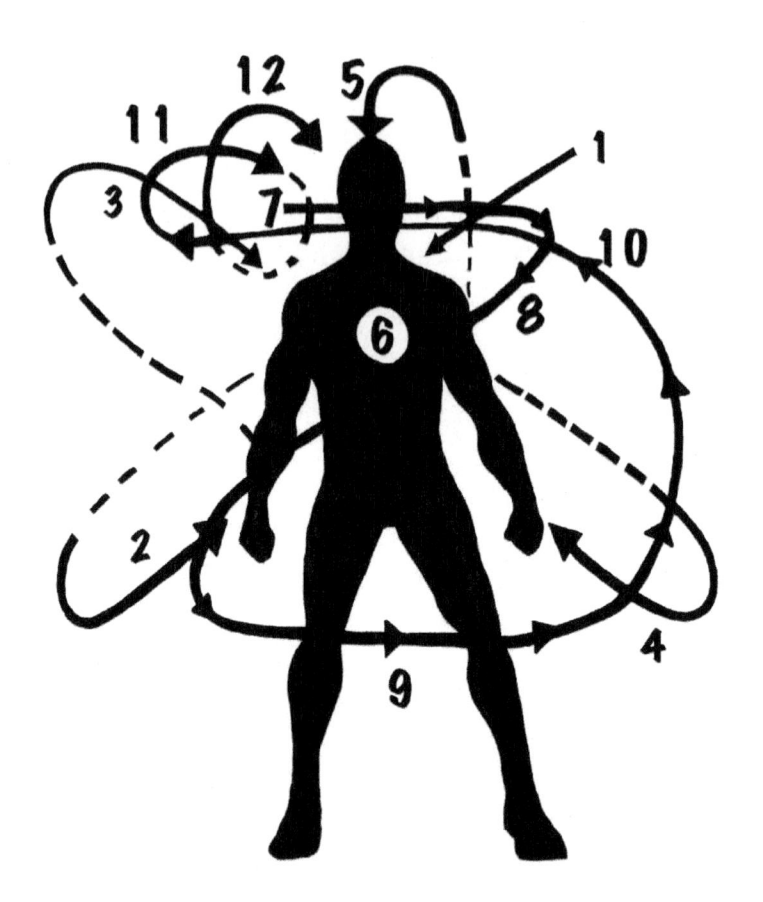

Twelve Angles of Attack (Fluid)

Angle #1- Downward diagonal strike to the opponent's left head, neck, or shoulder area. Flow completely through the body with the strike.

Angle #2- Upward diagonal strike to the opponent's right knee, hip, or side. After impact, flow up to the opponent's right side to prepare for angle three.

Angle #3- Downward diagonal strike to the opponent's right head, neck, or shoulder area. Flow completely through the body with the strike.

Angle #4- Upward diagonal strike to the opponent's left knee, hip, or side. After impact, flow straight up to prepare for angle five.

Angle #5- Straight downward strike to the opponent's head.

Angle #6- Straight strike or thrusting attack to the opponent's center.

Angle #7- High vertical strike from the opponent's right to left side, across the face or throat.

Angle #8- Downward diagonal strike from the opponent's left, across the midsection.

Angle #9- Low vertical strike from the opponent's right to left side, across the thighs or knees. Flow upward to prepare for angle ten.

Angle #10- High vertical strike from the opponent's left to right side, across the face or throat. Flow directly over for the angle eleven strike.

Angle #11- Downward whipping blow to the opponent's right-side temple or head. Pull back to flow into angle twelve.

Angle #12- Straight thrust high to the opponent's face or throat.

After you have learned the twelve angles of attack, you should start by practicing them from one to twelve in one fluid sequence without pausing between strikes. The angles can be attacked with any empty hand strike or with a weapon. For example, an angle ten strike is the same regardless of whether it is a hook punch, elbow strike, stick attack, or knife slash. To really feel the flow, I recommend using a bladed weapon such as a knife. Always practice with a dull training knife at first to avoid any accidental injuries.

When you can easily flow from angle one to angle twelve in a fluid manner, start mixing up the angles randomly without losing the flow. You could strike angle one and then flow right into angle three and then to angle eight. The combinations are almost limitless. The below sequence of photos shows the continuous flow of angles one through twelve with a knife.

Angle #1- Downward diagonal slash

Angle #2- Upward diagonal slash

Angle #3- Downward diagonal slash

Angle #4- Upward diagonal slash

Forging The Mind And Body

Angle #5- Downward slash

Angle #6- Straight Thrust

Angle #7- High horizontal slash

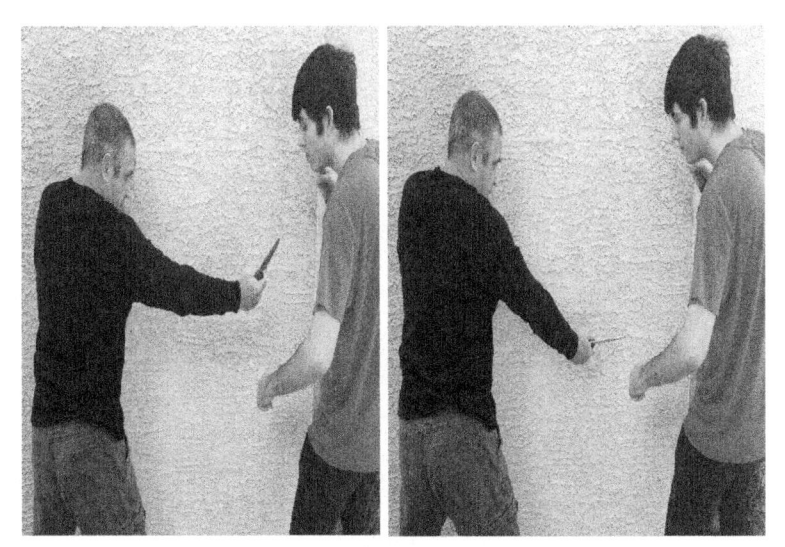

Angle #8- Downward slash

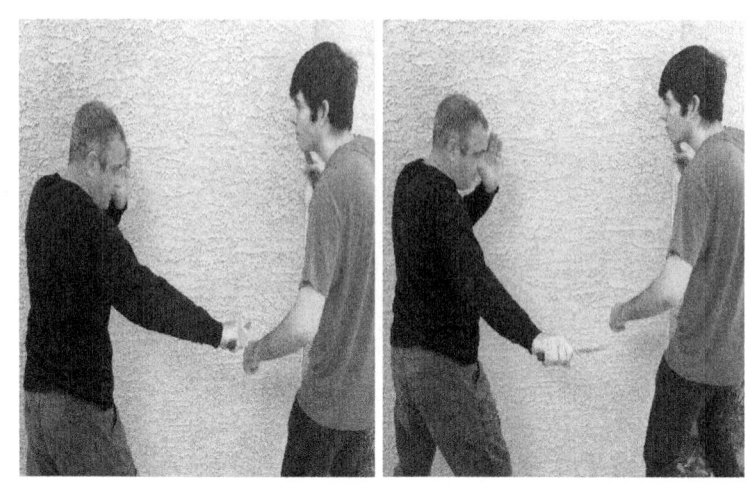

Angle #9- Low horizontal slash

Angle #10- High horizontal slash

Angle #11- Downward whipping strike

Angle #12- High diagonal thrust

Adapt and Flow Exercise Three
Defend the Twelve Angles

We will now take the previous exercise a step further by having your training partner strike at you along the twelve angles of attack, and you will defend and counterattack. Your training partner should start by attacking the angles at a moderate pace in order, from one through twelve. You will defend against each attack and launch one or two counter strikes before the next attack comes.

Once you become proficient, have your training partner increase the speed so that you have less time to counter strike between each attack. Eventually, your partner will be attacking so quickly that your only opportunity to counter will be with half beat strikes executed as you flow between defending against the incoming attacks.

The final phase of this exercise involves your training partner attacking randomly along the various angles. Again, your partner will start at a moderate pace and mix up the attacking angles as you defend and counter strike. As your skills increase, have your partner pick up the pace until eventually you are defending against full speed attacks. At this phase you will be forced to adapt, flow, and insert your counter strikes in between defending against your partner's strikes.

After a month or two of practicing this exercise, you will notice a big difference in your ability to defend against random attacks and flow with your attacker's movement. If you have done this exercise consistently with sticks or training knives, empty hand attacks will seem much slower and easier to deal with. The below photos show this drill being done with a knife.

Forging The Mind And Body

You slice the arm against an angle #1 attack

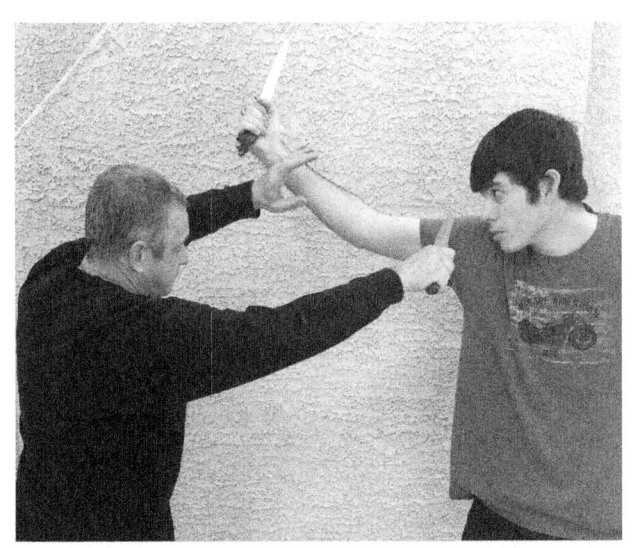

Immediately flow to an angle #7 slash

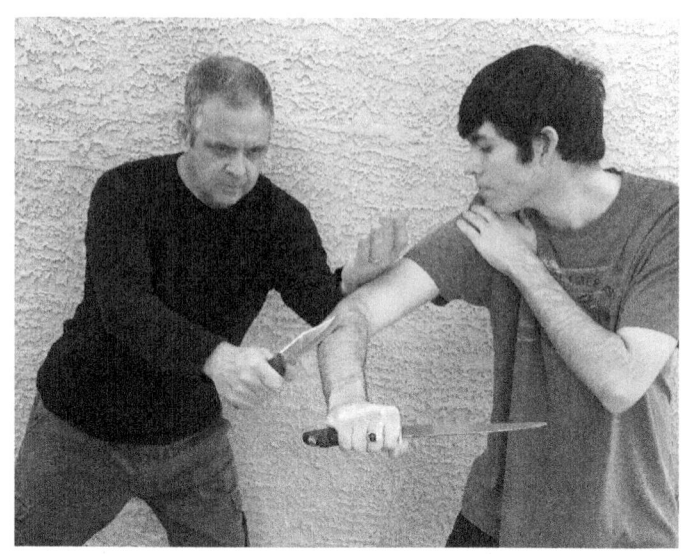

Parry and cut against an angle #7

Flow into an angle #6 thrust

Roof block and slash against Angle #5

Check and control the arm as you flow

Forging The Mind And Body

Slash angle #1

Parry and slash out against angle #2

Adapt and Flow Exercise Four
Carenza

Carenza is a form of shadow boxing that is used in the Filipino Martial Arts. It is an excellent exercise for developing flow and rhythm in your fighting techniques. Carenza is usually done with weapons, but it can also be practiced with empty hand techniques as well.

To perform the exercise, find a space where you won't be bothered and set an egg timer for two or three minutes. I recommend turning on some music to practice to. Traditionally this exercise was done to the beat of drums, but any music you like will do. Next, simply shadow spar for the duration of the egg timer.

Try to move with the rhythm of the music and flow from one technique to another in a fluid manner. Footwork is an extremely important part of proper flow. Avoid jerky or irregular movements during the exercise. As you execute your movements in a continuous manner, imagine that an opponent is blocking or countering your attack and you must flow immediately into another strike. Don't stop moving and flowing until the timer rings. You may repeat this exercise for as many rounds as you wish.

Once you have developed the ability to flow and adapt to whatever your opponent may do, you will have a skill that is extremely valuable for a martial artist.

The Point of No Return

The Point of No Return is a concept that has served me very well over the years. Once learned, it gives you the ability to make tough decisions in a split second, and to have the determination to follow through and accomplish tasks without second guessing yourself. Ironically, I first learned the Point of No Return Concept from my high school driver's training instructor.

It was my first lesson actually driving in the car with my instructor, so I was obviously very nervous. We pulled out onto the roadway and I began to slowly increase my speed to match the speed limit. I was traveling about forty-five miles per hour as I approached a traffic intersection, when suddenly the light changed from green to yellow.

I wasn't sure what I should do in that moment. I was pretty close to the intersection when the light changed, and I knew it would be red in a second. Should I slam on my brakes and risk sliding partially into the intersection, or should I accelerate and risk running the red light? I started to brake, but then changed my mind and started to accelerate. The light changed to red just as I went through it. The instructor told me to pull the car over to the side of the road. I was sure I was in major trouble, but what happened next turned out to be a powerful tool for me that I have used many times throughout my life.

The driving instructor said that sometimes in life you need to establish a point of no return. He told me that when the light had changed yellow, I wasn't sure what I should do. I started to stop, but then changed my mind and started to go faster. He said that as I approach intersections, I should identify something such as a light pole or a power box and use it as a point of no return. If the light changes to yellow before I reach the point of no return, I stop. If I reach the point of no return before the light changes to yellow, I will go. He finished his advice by saying that making a bad decision is always better than making no decision at all.

I began to use this principle when driving and soon discovered that I seldom slammed on my brakes at an intersection as the light changed suddenly. I also never ran any red lights. I either stopped easily before the light became red or made it through the intersection while it was still yellow. My point of no return made it easy for me to decide because it was already established in my mind.

I soon found that I was using this principle in other areas of my life beyond driving. If I recognized that a certain situation might occur, I would establish a point of no return in my mind where I would act based on a decision I had already thought out and made. The point of no return becomes a trigger to act so that there are no second thoughts or hesitation.

One example occurred when I was working the streets as a police officer, I responded to a call of a person who had attempted suicide and needed to be quickly transported to the hospital. The paramedics were on the scene and trying to get the man into the ambulance, but he wouldn't cooperate. When I arrived, he was moving around and throwing kicks and punches into the air. His wrists had been slit and he was bleeding profusely as the paramedics were trying to reason with him. Despite their efforts, the man wouldn't listen and just kept yelling and doing Kung-Fu like motions in the air.

The man didn't see me as I approached him from behind. I decided to set up a point of no return. As long as he did not move towards the paramedics with his attacks, I would simply observe and let them continue to talk with him. If on the other hand, he were to move towards them in a threatening manner, I would use physical force to subdue him. Any aggressive movement towards the paramedics would be my point of no return and would trigger my action.

After several minutes of negotiation with the man, it became evident that he would not comply with their directions to get into the ambulance. He was losing a lot of blood and still moving around erratically. At one point he started to move aggressively towards the paramedics and raised his leg to kick. That was my point of no return, so I immediately moved in from behind and subdued him. The paramedics were able to get him on a gurney and provide medical care which probably saved his life.

The key to the Point of No Return concept is to eliminate hesitation or failure to respond when a situation occurs that requires you to make a split-second decision. Establishing a line in the sand beforehand and having a plan in place for how you will respond to a situation, eliminates the need for decision making when seconds count. The practical application of this principle can be seen with the following hypothetical scenario.

You are in a sports bar having dinner with some friends when you accidently bump into another patron causing him to spill his beer. The person becomes extremely angry and begins to yell profanities at you. You try to de-escalate the situation and even offer to buy the gentleman another beer, but he continues to act aggressively and closes the distance between you.

In addition to being physically prepared with your body bladed and your hands up in a non-threatening manner, you establish a point of no return in your mind. As long as the aggressor exhibits verbal aggression only, you will continue to try and de-escalate the situation, but if he attempts to put his hands on you in any way such as a push or poke, you will instantly react.

Your reaction plan is entirely up to you, and will be based on numerous factors such as your training, the threat level, the environment, and the type of situation you are in. Your plan may be to strike with punches or kicks, to grapple with the opponent, or to utilize a weapon, all depending on the totality of the situation at hand. The key point here is to establish that clear line in the sand that will trigger you into action.

Often you will establish a point of no return and it will never be crossed. In the above scenario for example, the aggressor calms down after you replace his drink, and he walks away. There was obviously to need to defend yourself with physical force, but the point of no return concept gave you the clear reaction plan to act without hesitation if needed.

Sensitivity

Sensitivity is a valuable skill for a martial artist to possess. Unfortunately, it is often overlooked by fighters. When we hear the word "sensitivity", we often think of anything except the martial arts. We may think of hugging baby kittens or crying over a heart felt poem, but in the context of attributes for fighting, we are talking about something very different.

Sensitivity from a martial arts perspective involves being able to read and feel the movements and intentions of your opponent. When this skill is fully developed, you have more options available to you than simply meeting force with force. This is the classic concept of being able to redirect the attacker's energy and use his own force against him. It is this skill that enables a smaller and weaker person to defeat a much larger and stronger opponent.

To better understand how sensitivity can be developed, lets look at an analogy I like to use of driving on the freeway. It is a busy afternoon, and you are travelling down the freeway in heavy traffic. You suddenly get the feeling that the car in the lane next to you is going to cut over into your lane. As you start to slow down and watch the vehicle, it cuts over in front of you, exactly how you expected. You knew what the other driver was going to do before he did it.

If you have been driving for any length of time, I'm sure the above scenario has happened to you on numerous occasions. The question is, how did you know the car was going to cut you off? There were probably numerous clues that your mind noticed and instantly processed. It might have been the slight turn of the front wheels of the vehicle, or a quick head movement of the driver. It could have been a slight acceleration of the car, or the fact that another vehicle was travelling extremely slow ahead of him in his lane. Because you have experienced these indicators and the resulting outcome numerous times in the past, you were able to accurately predict its occurrence.

The problem is that we often don't listen to our gut instincts when they tell us something. How many times have you heard someone say, "something just didn't seem right", when talking about a bad situation that happened to them? In addition to subconscious clues we might ignore, we also have survival instincts that have been a part of us since the dawn of time. These survival instincts are similar to the one's animals have that alert them to danger. We have all heard the stories about animals seeking higher ground before a tsunami or acting funny before an earthquake. In order to develop our sensitivity to the fullest, we must learn to quit ignoring our gut feelings.

An additional thing to consider when perfecting your sensitivity skills is that they do not deteriorate with age like many other skills do. In fact, your sensitivity skills can continue to improve well into your senior years. In the remainder of this chapter, we will look at several exercises to increase your sensitivity in both listening to your survival instincts and reading your opponent's actions and energy. If you take the time to perfect these skills to their fullest, you will have a distinct advantage over the vast majority of adversaries you might encounter.

Sensitivity Exercise One
Trusting Your Gut

The purpose of this exercise is to train you to first recognize when your gut instincts are talking to you and then to have the confidence to act upon your instincts. Trust is obviously something that must be built over time (even when it involves your gut), so we will start slowly. You will practice this exercise the next time you go out in public.

The next time that you pull into a gas station or a shopping center parking lot, relax for a few moments before you get out of your car and look around the lot. Take notice of all of the things you might see around you that normally you would ignore such as a person sitting in their car, or someone approaching customers. Are there any individuals loitering around the lot or looking into car windows? What does your gut tell you about each person you see?

Listen to your instincts as you take notice of everything that's going on around you. While you are watching people move around the shopping center, try to make predictions about what they will do, based on your gut instincts. Will they get into a certain car or go into a specific store? Will they join up with anyone else, or are they alone? As you observe, see how many of your predictions come true.

The ultimate goal here is to take the time to become aware of your surroundings, and then listen to what your gut tells you about your surroundings. Then finally to see how often your gut instincts were right. This exercise can be performed anyplace where there are people but be sure and do it in a casual manner, so you don't creep out people or bring unwanted attention to yourself. Again, casual awareness of your surroundings.

You can even make a game out of this exercise with your kids while waiting for your spouse in a shopping mall or while eating in a food court. Simply make observations and predictions such as, "I'll bet the guy in the red shirt goes into the sunglasses store", or "The lady with the baby stroller will order Chinese Food." Then see how often your predictions come true. Remember that the key is to listen to what your gut tells you, and not just to make random bets.

The next phase of this exercise will be to listen to your gut instincts when dealing with people. If you are negotiating with a car salesman, dealing with a solicitor, or having a conversation with a co-worker, ask yourself what your instincts are telling you about the situation. Is the person truthful or are they lying? Do they have your best interests in mind, or do they have ulterior motives? Ultimately, to develop this skill to a high level you must accomplish two things. First, listen to what your instincts are telling you, and second, pay attention to when they are correct.

Using the opponent's force against him

Developing your sensitivity goes well beyond learning to trust your gut instincts. You must also be able to develop your physical skills to recognize your opponent's movements and respond appropriately to the force he applies against you. By appropriately harnessing your opponent's force, you will be able to easily double the power of your own attacks.

We have all experienced the odd situation where you reach to push open a door and at the same time someone opens the door from the other side. This usually results in you tumbling forward until you are able to regain your balance. Think of that feeling of surprise you had when you momentarily lost your stability and control for just a brief moment. That is exactly the situation you want to be able to use against your opponent.

We can simplify the types of force your opponent can exert when attacking you into six categories. These categories are as follows.

Types of force
1) Forward force (Push)
2) Backward force (Pull)
3) Upward Force (Lift)

4) Downward force (Press down)
5) Sideways force
6) No force

Each of these types of force can each be displayed in different manners or in various combinations. For example, the opponent could strike with a straight punch which is forward force. He might also push you, or shoot in for a takedown, which are also types of forward force. A pull, a strike to the rear, or rear sacrifice throw, are all examples of backwards force. Although each type of force might require a different response, knowing how to harness or disperse the force will follow the same general process, regardless of the type of force used.

The main principle is to avoid meeting force with direct force. Lets again use the analogy of driving a vehicle. If you were driving down the road and suddenly ran into a brick wall, the result would be devastating. You would probably be severely injured, your car totaled, and the wall destroyed. Now imagine that instead of hitting a wall, you were to strike another vehicle coming at you head on. Obviously, the results of the second collision would be much more devastating because you have two objects moving with substantial force, meeting each other head on.

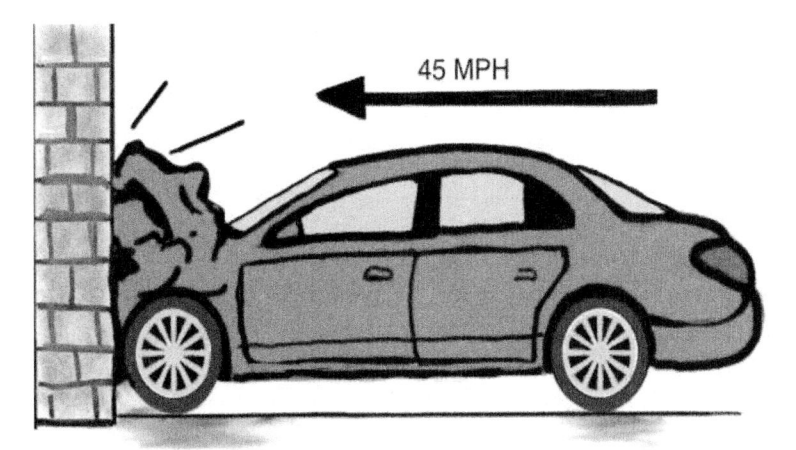

Stationary Wall

Force Against Force

Now think of the first collision scenario again, but this time imagine there is a large puddle of oil in the street in front of the wall. As the car approaches the wall at high speed, the front wheels hit the oil and begin to slide. The oil spill acts as an outside force and redirects the forward energy of the vehicle slightly. As a result, the car might miss the wall completely. If it does hit the wall, the impact will be considerably less than it would have been when all of the force of the vehicle was moving forward.

Brick Wall

Incoming Force Is Redirected

Oil Spill Acts As An Outside Force

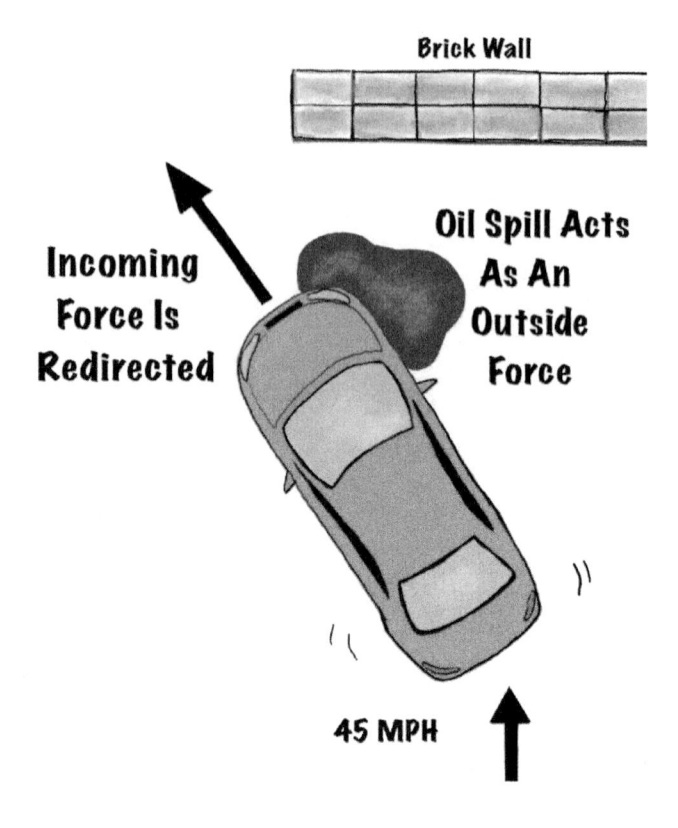

45 MPH

You might be asking yourself how this all applies to improving your fighting skills. The trick is to develop your sensitivity to the point where you instantly recognize the type of force your opponent is using against you, and then redirect his force the same way the puddle of oil redirected the force of the vehicle. The following exercise will give you a basic foundation to work from.

Sensitivity Exercise Two
Join the Force

To perform this exercise, you will start from a high contact point with your training partner. A contact point is made anytime your arm contacts the opponent's arm during a fight. This commonly occurs when the opponent blocks a punch you have thrown, or when you block an attack from the opponent. This is also sometimes referred to as a bridge. The basic high contact point that you will use for this exercise is shown in the below photo.

From the High contact point, your training partner will apply one of the six types of force against your arm. He might push into you or retract his hand. He might move your arm to the side or press your arm down. He could also lift up on your arm or simply do nothing at all. Regardless of what he does, you will react to control and redirect his energy. For this exercise, we will give you a simple response for each type of force.

The High Bridge or Contact Point

Forward Force- From the high contact point, your training partner pushes forward against your arm. You redirect his force by grabbing his wrist and pulling him into a strike. Just like the two vehicles colliding head on, his forward force in conjunction with the pulling of his arm, causes your strike to hit him with multiplied power. In the below photos, the training partner uses forward force from the high contact point. The practitioner feels the forward energy and instead of resisting, goes with it. He grabs the partner's wrist as he redirects the attack and counters with a rear cross.

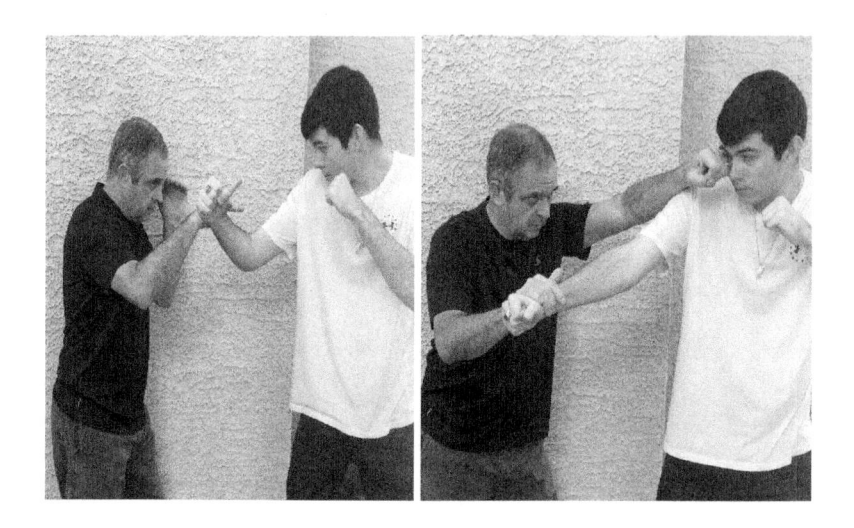

Backward Force- This time your training partner grabs your wrist and pulls you forward using backward force. Rather than resist his pull, you move in with his force as you strike. As with the previous example, his pull combined with your forward momentum, greatly increases the power of your attack. In the below photos, the training partner grabs the practitioner's wrist from the high contact point and pulls him forward as he prepares to strike. The practitioner goes with the force of the pull by moving in and immediately striking with a cross.

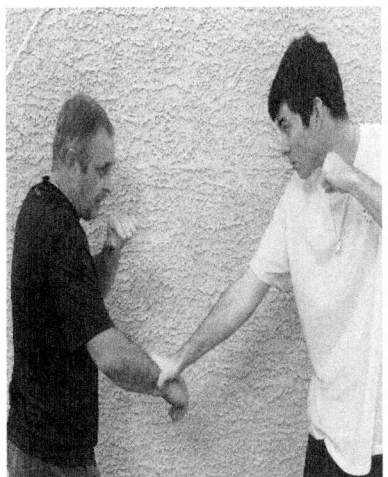

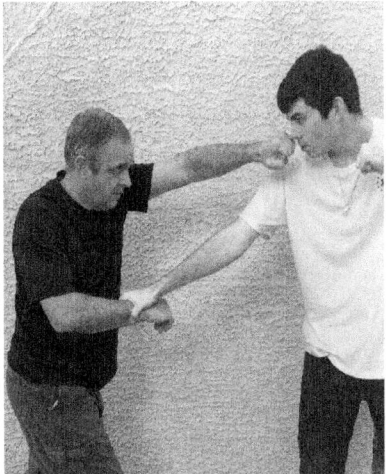

Upward Force- When your training partner provides upward force and attempts to lift your arm, go with his force until it dissipates, then immediately circle your arm back to counter or defend. In most cases, if the opponent uses upward energy, he is trying to create a low opening to attack, so be ready for this. In the below sequence of photos, the training partner uses upward force from the high contact point to lift the practitioner's arm. The practitioner responds by going with the force and attacking low to the body. He closely monitors the practitioner's rear hand.

Downward Force- If your training partner uses downward force, and tries to push your arm straight down, go with his motion and lower your arm with his force until it starts to dissipate. Flow into a counterstrike using the momentum of his force, then quickly circle your hands back to defend yourself. In the below photos, the training partner uses downward force to push the practitioner's arm downward. The practitioner goes with the downward energy until it dissipates, then he attacks to the partner's head with an open palm strike while checking the lead arm.

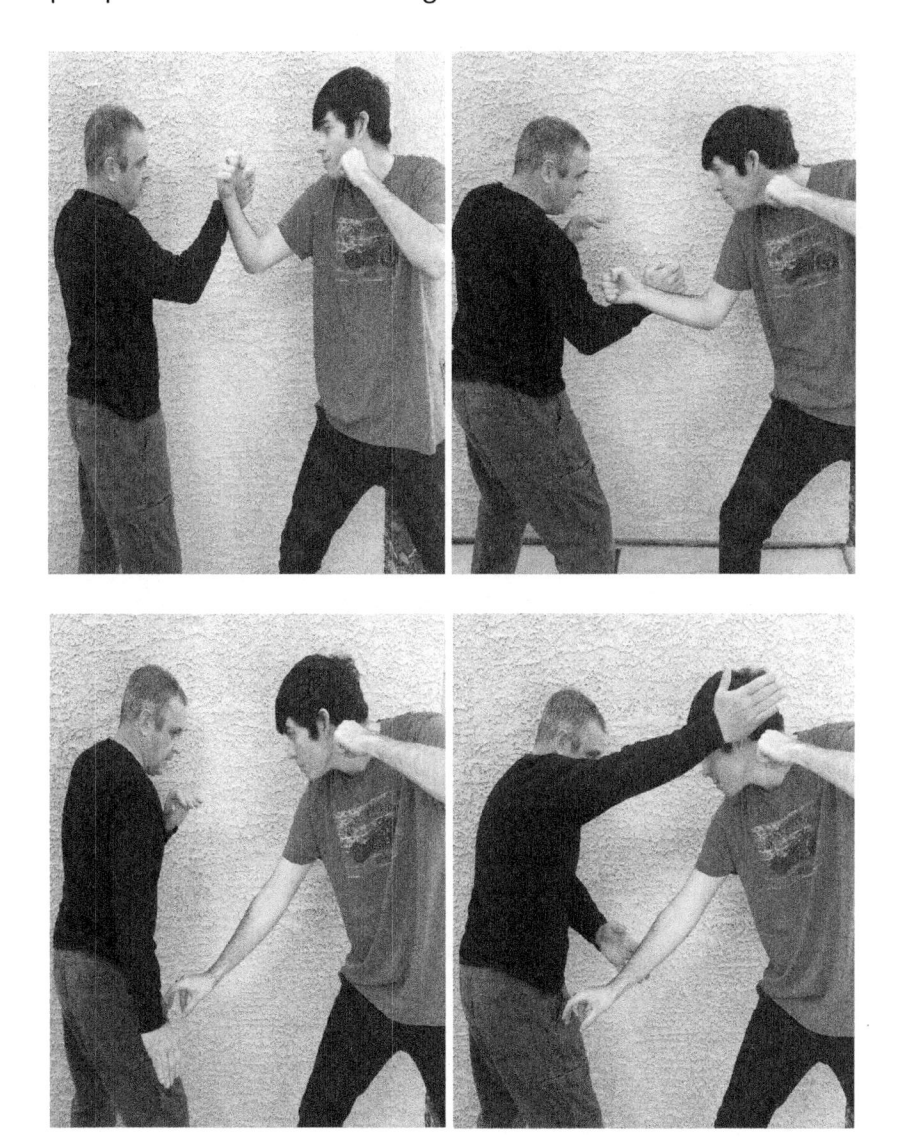

Sideways Force- After the high contact point is made, your training partner tries to force your arm to one side or the other. You respond by collapsing your arm in the direction of his force rather than resisting. You may then counterattack as you wish. In the example shown below, the training partner applies sideways force against the practitioner's arm. He collapses his arm at the elbow to go with the direction of the force and rolls his arm into a back fist attack.

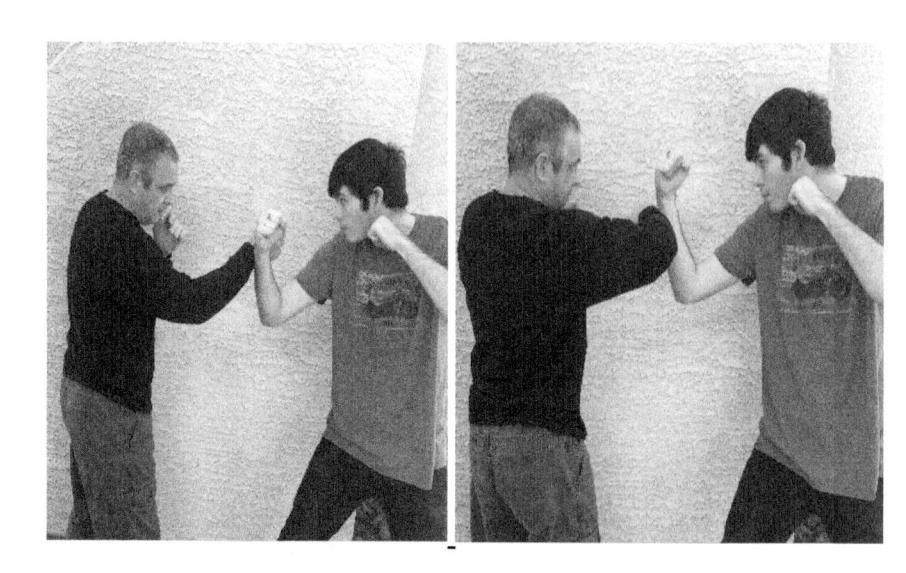

No Force- When your training partner makes contact but gives you no force at all, you can simply check his arm in place and instantly attack. Because he applies no force against you, you are free to counter as you wish. The reality is that it is very rare for an opponent to make contact and not respond with some type of force once an encounter has begun.

The important part of this exercise is not the counterattack, but rather feeling your training partner's direction of force and redirecting it. In addition to redirecting the opponent's force, many times you can join with his force and use it to your advantage. There are numerous examples of how this concept can be employed in fighting techniques. One classic example of this is a clothesline attack, where you redirect an opponent's force, follow his force to increase his momentum, and then put your arm right across his throat to clothesline him.

Sensitivity Exercise Three
Drawing the opponent's Force

It is a natural human reaction to use force against force. In this exercise we will practice using that natural reaction against your opponent by drawing his force. This concept is commonly used in Judo and wrestling and involves baiting your opponent by giving him a certain type of force, and then using his resistance against him.

To start, face your training partner and cross arms to establish a high contact point. From this position you will give your training partner one of the six types of force. Your force should be slightly exaggerated in order to solicit a response from your training partner. Most untrained fighters will respond to force with opposite force. For example, if you push the opponent with forward force, he will usually respond by pushing back with backward force. Based on this, for the first phase of this exercise your partner will respond with opposite force.

When your training partner responds with force opposite to the force you have used, you will resist slightly, then instantly collapse your resistance and go with his counter force exactly like you did in the previous exercise. The difference is that in the first exercise you received force and then redirected it. In this exercise you give force, receive the counter force, and then redirect it.

Once you become proficient responding to opposite force, have your training partner counter with a random force. For example, you apply forward force, your partner counters with sideways force, you redirect his sideways force. Eventually you will be able to respond instantly to any type of force your opponent uses against you, bait your opponent into using a certain force, and respond accordingly when he doesn't use the type of force you expected. This is a very valuable skill for any fighter to have.

To take these exercises to a higher level, expand your practice beyond the contact point exercise. Practice redirecting force from a clinch position, from strikes, grappling, and finally during sparring sessions. This exercise can also be done with weapons such as sticks or training knives. Classical fencing and sword fighting masters utilized these concepts a great deal in their training. Start off slowly at first and gradually increase your speed and power as you become more efficient in these exercises.

The below series of photographs show an example of this type of training being employed. The training partner and practitioner start in a classic grappling clinch. The practitioner applies forward force against the training partner by pushing him backwards. When the training partner resists, and pushes back with his own forward force, the practitioner goes with his forward energy and executes a shoulder throw. Although this technique is a basic technique that is commonly used in the art of Judo, many practitioners overlook the higher-level skill of soliciting your opponent's force and then capitalizing on it.

Example #1
Drawing Force from the Clinch

From a clinch position, the defender pushes forward against the opponent to solicit a response. When the opponent pushes back against his force, he collapses his structure and uses the opponent's forward energy to flow right into a shoulder throw.

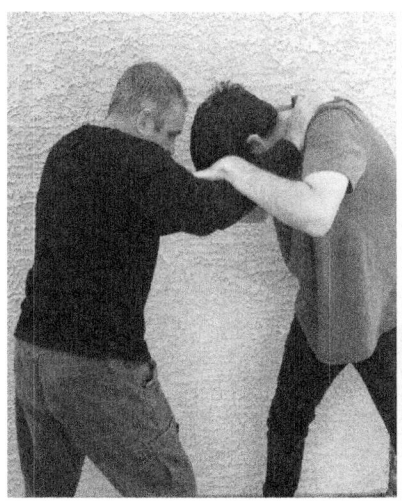

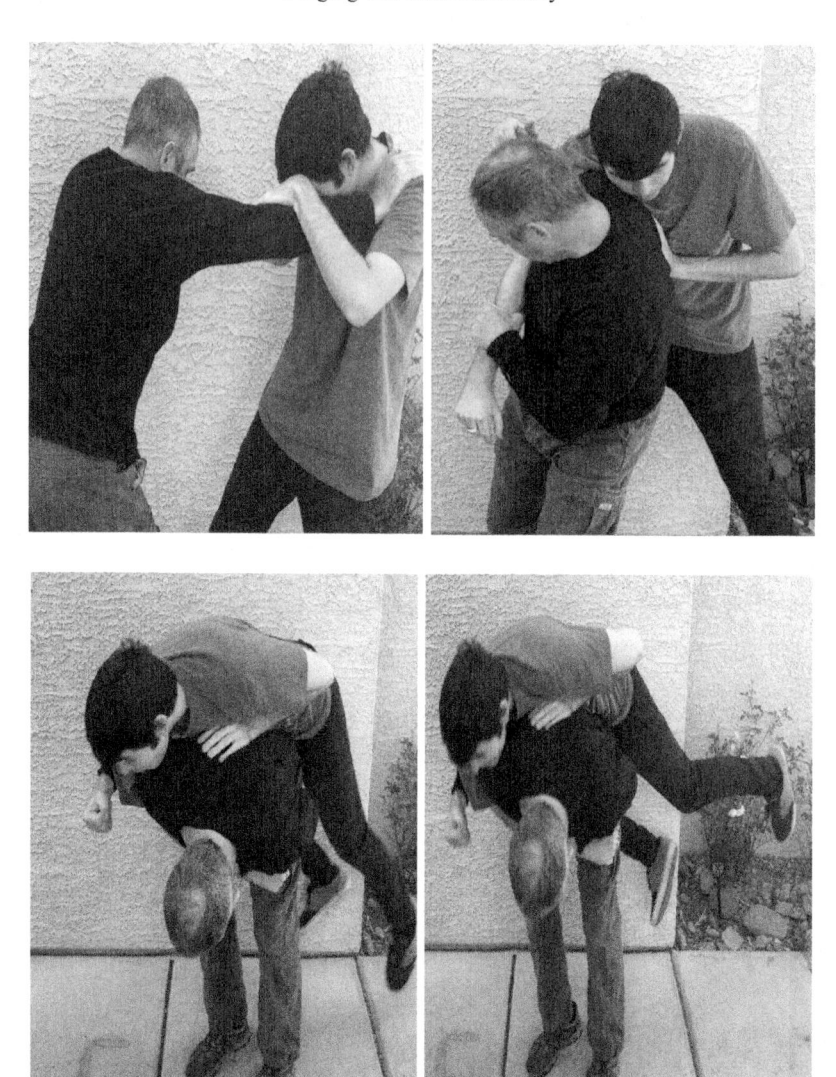

The following example uses the same principle but employs a striking attack instead of a throw. The practitioner starts the exchange by pushing his training partner backwards. The training partner immediately resists the push by applying his own forward force back towards the practitioner. The practitioner responds by going with the incoming force and rotating his body inward as he steps off line of the attack. This causes the training partner to suddenly lose his balance and stumble forward just like the example of pushing a door open as someone opens it from the opposite side. The practitioner uses this opportunity to attack the back of the partner's neck with a hammer fist or elbow strike.

Example #2

The defender pushes the opponent backwards to solicit a response. When the opponent responds with forward force, he redirects his energy to the side and executes a strike to the back of his neck.

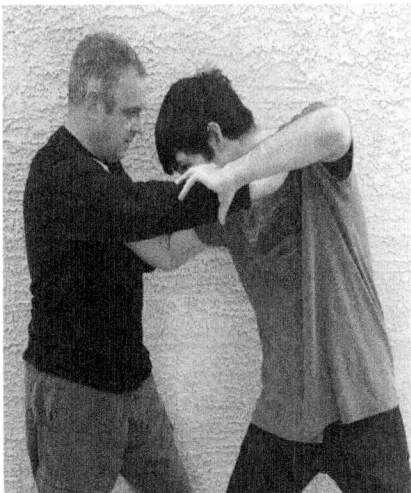

Forging The Mind And Body

Tension/Sealing the Gates

In today's day and age, the term tension usually has a negative connotation. We tend to think of tension in the same category as stress, anxiety, or stiffness. When studying martial arts and other sports there is an emphasis on relaxation in order to obtain optimal performance. While there is truth to all of this, tension is not always a bad thing. When properly used, tension can be a valuable tool for the advanced martial artist.

The ancient martial arts masters knew the value of properly applied tension for combat. This can be seen in the numerous traditional forms and kata that contain movements which are performed while tensing portions of the body. The Okinawan kata called Sanchin is just one classic example of this. Why did the ancient masters place an emphasis on tension in certain movements and techniques? There are a number of reasons that we will explore.

Ability to absorb an attack

As we discussed in the chapter on breathing, exhaling, and tensing the body when receiving a blow from the opponent can help minimize the damage of the strike. You have probably heard the story of the famous magician Harry Houdini who would have people strike him in the stomach during his performances to demonstrate his ability to withstand a blow. Depending on the version of the legend you read, Houdini was resting backstage when he was struck in the stomach by an audience member who wanted to test his ability. Because Houdini was not prepared for the blow, he suffered injury which may have contributed to his death.

Although tension can be very useful when defending against blows to the body, the problem is that sustained tension causes fatigue and slows you down. The key is to remain relaxed until the exact moment that tension is needed and then immediate tense the body. As soon as tension is no longer needed, it is instantly released. When tension is employed at the correct time, you can conserve energy, remain relaxed, retain speed, and still protect your body against incoming blows.

In some cases, tensing the body at the proper time can even be a counter offensive technique. I have witnessed fighters injure themselves and even break a wrist while punching someone who instantly tensed their body just as the strike made impact. I have also seen sudden tension used to knock an opponent backwards. This isn't some mystical chi power, but rather a physical technique.

Tension Exercise One
Sealing the Nine Gates

Years ago, when I was studying Kung-Fu, my sifu taught me an exercise called sealing the nine gates of the body. I was told that this exercise has its origins in the ancient Iron Shirt systems that were designed to make the human body impervious to attacks. This is a simple exercise that can be performed any where and will give you the ability to instantly tense areas of the body so you can successfully absorb attacks. Before we get into specifics of the exercise, keep in mind that using tension to absorb an attack should be considered a last resort. You should always use other methods of defense as your primary means to deal with attacks.

For the purposes of this exercise, the human body has nine gates which can be sealed to protect against an opponent's strike.

To get a mental image of this concept, think of an ancient city that is surrounded by a large wall to protect the inhabitants. At certain places in the wall there are gates that allow the citizens of the city to come and go as they please, but when the city is under siege, the gates can be sealed to protect against the invaders. Just like the gates in the city wall, the gates of the body can be sealed for protection. The nine gates of the body are as follows.

Nine Gates of the Body
1) Ankles
2) Knees
3) Groin
4) Abdomen
5) Chest
6) Wrists
7) Elbows
8) Neck
9) Teeth/Jaw

Start the exercise by standing with your feet shoulders width apart. Take a step forward with your right foot and turn your toes inward forty-five degrees. There should be about a foots distance between the feet. Bend your knees inward towards each other and raise your arms in front of your body with your fists clinched. The fists are held at shoulder level with the elbows pointed inwards. Your arms are bent at a forty-five-degree angle with the fists clenched and protruding just slightly outside of the line of the shoulders. Tuck your chin slightly and look forward. Keep the back rounded and the tailbone tucked slightly. This is the classic hourglass position. From this position we will begin sealing the nine gates.

Forging The Mind And Body

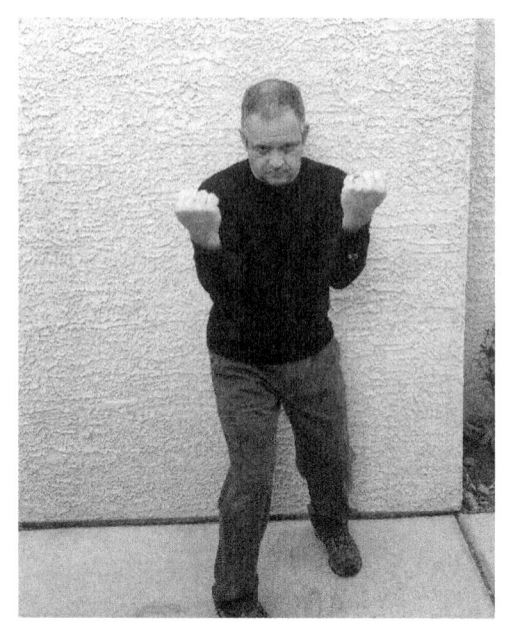

The Hourglass Position (Front)

The Hourglass Position (Side)

In the first phase of this exercise, we will start sealing the gates from the ground up. Begin by gripping the ground with your toes and feet, similar to a suction cup. Feel the arch of your foot rise as the rest of the foot cups the ground. You are now ready to seal each gate moving up the body in the following order.

Ankles- Physically tighten your ankles and feel the ankle joints lock up as if your shin bone and foot have just become a solid object. As you seal the gates, imagine they are being filled with concrete that is rapidly solidifying. Hold this tension as you move to the next gate.

Knees- Rising up from the ankles, tighten the knee joints and force them slightly closer together. The leg is now tense from the thighs down to the feet and should feel like one solid unit, similar to the trunk of an oak tree.

Groin- With the first two gates successfully sealed, you will now move to the groin area. This area actually encompasses more than just the groin itself and includes the waist, anus, and hip joints. While maintaining the seal of the first two gates, tighten your groin, anal sphincter, and hip joints. Allow the groin to sink inward below the upper thighs as you tighten the area. Your waist also tightens. At this point, your entire lower body from the waist down is tense and tightened up into one solid structure.

Abdomen- With the lower body sealed, now you will tighten up the abdomen. Feel the muscles in the abdominal wall tense and come together to protect your internal organs. Be sure to tighten the midsection around your entire body, and not just the abdomen muscles themselves.

Chest- Continuing up the body, you will now seal the chest and upper back. Again, tighten the chest muscles, and your latissimus dorsi muscles to seal this section of your body. Continue to hold all of the previous gates sealed as well.

Wrists- In the same fashion that you sealed the ankles, you will now seal the wrists. Tense the wrist joints and tighten the forearm muscles until your upper arms feel like a solid structure.

Elbows- From the wrists and forearms, lock the elbows and tense the remainder of the arms up to the shoulders. Your entire body from the neck down is now one solid mass. It is tense and locked in place to protect your vital targets.

Neck- The neck now tenses and seals. You should feel the tendons and muscles in the neck tighten up and imagine your voice box sinking slightly in for protection.

Teeth/Jaw- The final gate to seal is the teeth/jaw area. Clinch the teeth together and tighten the jaw to protect the lower face. The tension wraps around to include the back of your neck as well.

The Nine Gates

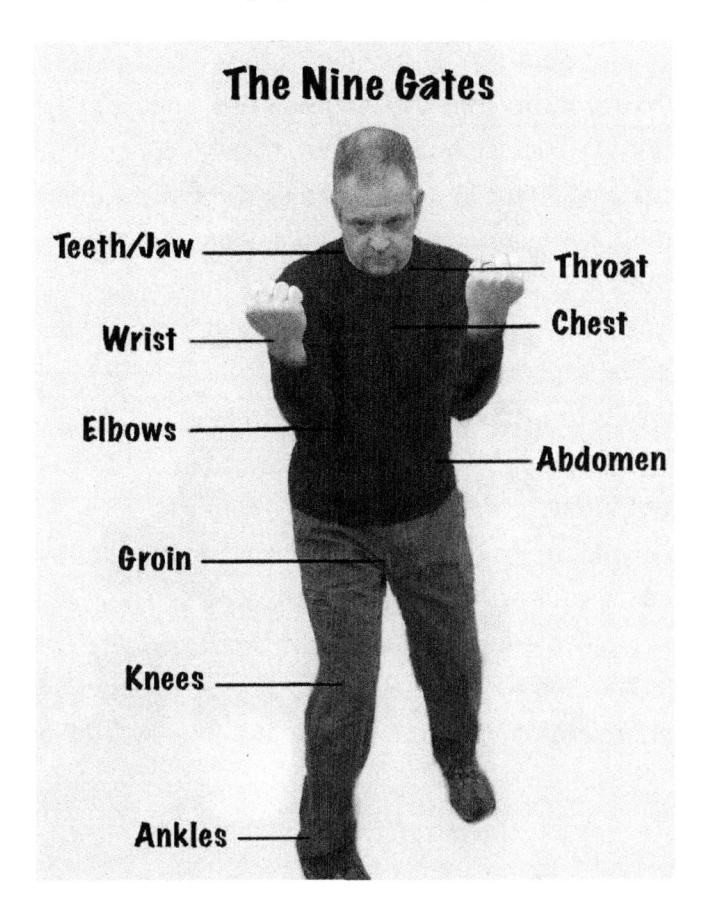

- Teeth/Jaw
- Throat
- Wrist
- Chest
- Elbows
- Abdomen
- Groin
- Knees
- Ankles

At this point you have successfully sealed all nine gates. Hold this position for a few seconds, and then begin to release the tension and open the gates one at a time. In the beginning, release tension and open the gates from the ground up in the same order that you sealed them. If you have taken the time to perform this exercise as described, you have seen how difficult and strenuous it can be to maintain the tension in your body as you seal the gates.

After you have become proficient in sealing the gates, have your training partner test your structure to make sure it is solid. Repeat the above exercise, but once all of the gates are sealed, hold the position while your training partner strikes your body to ensure the gates are closed and providing proper protection. Caution should be used during this phase of practice. I recommend using a padded training stick, or boxing gloves to test your structure. After a lot of practice, you can advance to lighter gloves, or sticks with less padding. My instructor used to use a bamboo Kendo training sword to test my structure.

After a month or two of practice, you will find that you are able to seal all nine gates almost instantly. You will also be able to release the gates instantly. Your ability to take shots to your body will have greatly increased. It is important to note that sealing the gates is not intended to replace proper defensive skills. You must train your blocks, parries, and evasion skills, and use these techniques as your primary means to defend yourself. Sealing the gates is a supplement and a last resort technique. For example, if you were knocked to the ground by an angry crowd who were kicking and punching you, you could seal the gates to help protect you from their attacks.

Tension Exercise Two
Advanced Sealing the Gates

In this second exercise for sealing the nine gates, we will take the previous exercise to the next level. Start by assuming the hourglass position as before, but this time you will seal the gates in random order. You may start by sealing the neck and then seal the knees. You might seal the chest followed by the teeth and jaw. At first, seal each gate at random and hold each of the nine gates until they are all sealed, then release each gate at random.

Next you will seal one of the nine gates and release it before you seal the next gate. As you can see, the combinations are almost limitless. For example, you could seal three gates and release two, or seal eight gates and release four. Ultimately your goal will be to instantly seal any of the nine gates at the moment an opponent attacks you.

Tension to help you relax

Ironically, tension can be a useful tool to assist you with relaxing during meditation, or prior to sleep. Just like the Chinese symbols for Yin and Yang complement each other, tension and relaxation also complement each other. Think about it for a moment, relaxation could not exist without tension, and vice versa. The following exercise has been very beneficial to me over the years for quickly reducing stress. I usually perform it just before bed.

Tension Exercise Three
Tense and Relax

I believe this exercise is most effective when performed while lying down, however you could practice it standing or sitting as well. Start by relaxing your entire body and surveying yourself from head to toe. Notice areas where you still have tension even though you are trying to relax. Most often these areas are in your neck, back, face, or arms. The tension in these areas can become so common that you may grow accustom to it over time. In some cases, you won't even notice the tension until you really pay close attention to it.

Once you have identified those areas in your body that still have tension, rather than struggle to relax them further, you are actually going to tense them more. If the tension is in your back, tighten your back muscles and tense up as much as you can for about five seconds, then release the tension. Notice how it feels when you let the tension go. Feel the muscles become loose and almost hang from your bones. Let the old tension go with the new tension when it is released. If you still feel a degree of tension after relaxing, relax a little further to release it.

When you reach the point where you can't relax any further, tense your muscles again and repeat the exercise as described. Eventually, the added tension and release will help you let go of the lingering tension you were experiencing. It will gradually dissipate along with the tension you purposely created and released.

If you can't identify any specific underlying tension in your body, you can use this exercise to release general tension from the entire body. While lying down, proceed as above, but instead of tensing a specific targeted area, tense the entire body. Hold the tension for about five seconds and then released it. Feel every muscle in your body become loose and relaxed. After a couple of repetitions of this exercise, you should have an easier time drifting off to sleep.

Tension to build strength

Because tension causes resistance in your muscles and tendons, it can be used to increase your overall strength. In fact, using tension to help build strength causes your muscles to have a strong but elastic quality that is different from the strength you develop from other methods such as lifting weights. Again, this is not a new concept. It is an age-old training method that was often employed by the ancient martial arts masters. The following exercise can easily be incorporated into your daily training regime to increase your overall strength.

Tension Exercise Four
Tension to Build Strength

To perform this exercise, pick a technique or a martial arts form you normally practice. Instead of executing the technique or form at normal speed, do it slowly with tension and resistance throughout the movements. If you are simply practicing a lead punch or a back-fist strike, the exercise will focus, specifically on those movements. Throw the technique extremely slow as if someone has cupped your fist and is pushing back on your hand as you strike.

If there is a traditional martial arts form or kata that you practice, it can become an excellent strength training exercise by incorporating tension into every movement. In addition to tensing your arm or leg as you execute strikes, tense the entire body in a manner similar to sealing the gates. Executing traditional kata at full speed, followed by very slowly with tension on every move is an extremely powerful exercise.

Another simple way to use this principle is to use one of your limbs to apply pressure and resistance against the other limb. For example, grab your own wrist with your opposite hand and push downward as you curl inward with the opposite arm. The two arms working against each other will create tension that exercises the muscles in your arms.

The main goal with all of the exercises in this chapter is to use tension to your advantage to strengthen the body and to protect against potential attacks. When you learn to harness tension and capitalize on its benefits, you will have an easier time achieving relaxation as well.

Conquering Fear

Fear is an extremely powerful force that can freeze us in our tracks or cause us to do things that are unimaginable. Consider how powerful fear must be to cause a person to leap to their death from a high-rise building to avoid the flames of a burning fire.

Although fear is a natural reaction to danger, the problem is that we never know how it will affect us until it strikes. This is the reason why seasoned military personnel or cops are often leery of the new guy who has not proven himself under fire.

Normal training alone does not reduce fear when a violent encounter occurs. We have all heard stories of highly trained individuals who froze under the pressure of a real situation. The good news is that there are ways you can tailor your training and prepare yourself to conquer fear when it comes calling.

Experience

One of the best ways to conquer the fear of something is to force yourself to do it. The more you engage in an activity, the more comfortable you become with being uncomfortable and the fear eventually goes away. In my current job I am required to do a lot of public speaking and testimony before the legislature. When I first started, I was terrified to get up in front of law makers and a room full of people to speak. I remember my hands literally shaking and my voice cracking as I approached the podium, but after time, my fear subsided.

Obviously as a martial artist you don't want to go out looking for fights in order to reduce your fear, however you can increase the intensity of your training to simulate a real situation more closely. By introducing more active resistance and physical contact into your practice sessions, and getting out of your comfort zone, you will see drastic improvements in your self confidence and fear reduction.

Conquering Fear Exercise One
Confronting Fear Head On

For this exercise, you will first identify a fear that is not related to martial arts, and face it head on. Next you will use this same principle to improve your martial arts skills. Start by identifying something that scares you. Be honest with yourself and pick something that you typically would avoid due to fear. It could be fear of heights, fear of snakes, fear of public speaking, or fear of approaching your boss for a raise. It really doesn't matter what fear you choose as long as it is a genuine fear.

Once you have identified a fear to tackle, you will arrange to do the very thing that scares you. For example, if fear of heights was your choice, pick a location where you can face this fear head on. You might take a trip to the Grand Canyon or go to the top of a skyscraper. Force yourself to face your fear head on. Once you have done it, don't stop there. Make a new habit of going to high locations that previously you would have avoided. Soon you will see the fear you had start to dwindle away.

You may also approach this exercise in graduated steps such as going to the top floor of an enclosed building first, and then after time going to an outdoor roof top. When this becomes less fearful to you, you could go to a high location with no protective railing, such as a cliff edge. Eventually, you might go so far as to sign up for sky diving lessons. The sky is literally the limit!

Conquering Fear Exercise Two
Get Out of Your Comfort Zone

Now we will apply this same concept to your martial arts training. The goal is simply to get out of your comfort zone and challenge yourself by facing your fears head on. Among the biggest fears we all tend to have are the fear of failure and fear of looking bad to our peers. These fears keep us from taking chances that result in positive change in our lives. I have seen numerous black belts who refuse to train in any other fighting systems because they don't want to put on a white belt again and be seen as a beginner. Once we are able to overcome these basic fears, we can then start to grow tremendously as martial artists.

The first thing you should do to get out of your comfort zone is to find martial artists who are better than you and train with them. If you only train with your own students, or people with equal skill, you will eventually reach a plateau that is very difficult to overcome. Pick an area of your martial arts skill set that you know needs significant improvement. Maybe it's your ground fighting skills, your boxing techniques, or weapons skills. Then get out and find a school that trains in that area and pay them a visit. Most martial arts schools will allow you to sit in on a class or two, and to train with their students. When you identify the people at the school who are really good. Approach them and ask them to train with you.

Some of the biggest wake up calls and advancements in my own martial arts training came after reaching out and being invited to train with others. I once approached a small group of guys who where stick fighting in the local park. My willingness to contact them and my genuine desire to learn, led to new friends and years of training with those guys, learning Arnis, Kenpo, and Tai Chi.

On rare occasion, the people you find in your search to get out of your comfort zone might actually be less skilled than you are. If this happens, don't just abandon them. Share your knowledge to help them grow along their martial arts path. Some of those same individuals might surpass you in skill down the road and repay the favor. The bottom line is, to improve your skill, you have to constantly put yourself to the test and seek new challenges. This means overcoming your fear of failure and embarrassment once and for all.

Working through fear

A common theme among people who have survived a life-or-death encounter is that they were scared to death, but they knew something had to be done immediately, so they acted. I was once told that when your life is at stake, it is better to take the wrong action, than to take no action at all. At any rate, you cannot allow fear to control you or stop you from doing what you know must be done.

One of the biggest obstacles to action is the fear that you will fail and get seriously injured, killed, or cause someone who you care about to get hurt or killed. This fear is often powerful enough to cause you to hesitate or worse, freeze up and fail to act when your life depends on it.

To respond properly when needed, you must be able to shut off the mental chatter that fuels the fear in your mind. This will not necessarily eliminate the fear, but it will allow you to clear your mind and focus on the task. The following mental exercise will give you the ability to overcome the internal fear of being injured or killed.

Conquering Fear Exercise Two
Fight Through the Fear

The purpose of this exercise is to create a mental trigger that will ignite your killer instinct to the point where fear is no longer a factor in your decision making. Before we begin, imagine the scene of a Moro warrior, who even after being shot numerous times, continues to charge, and kill his adversaries before succumbing to his wounds. The mind set that you will accomplish your goal with no concern for your own personal safety is the ultimate purpose of this exercise.

Another way to look at this mind set is the comment I have heard seasoned street fighters make over the years, "You might succeed in kicking my ass, but I'm gonna make sure you remember this fight everyday when you look in the mirror!"

To begin the exercise, stand in front of a heavy bag or some other striking target. Close your eyes and image the feeling you would have if someone had harmed your family or loved ones. Also think about the last time that you were completely enraged over something in your life. Let those feelings of rage and anger surface inside of you. Imagine that you no longer care about anything except taking the fight to the person who has caused your family harm. You are pissed off and want blood. The anger is boiling inside of you to the point where you are ready to explode.

Now pick a trigger word that you will use to instantly unleash all of your anger. When you say that trigger word in your mind, you will explode into the heavy bag or target with every ounce of fury you possess. Your only goal is to stop the threat and defeat your assailant with no concern for your own safety. The only way to stop you is to kill you and you have no fear of death. After about thirty seconds of nonstop aggression being released on your heavy bag or striking target. Stop and catch your breath.

Relax for a moment and gather your thoughts. Let that feeling you had of total aggression with no fear sink in. Take notice of the freedom you gained when all of your fearful thoughts were gone and only your killer instinct was leading the charge. Repeat this exercise until you are able to trigger your aggressive response instantly if needed.

Show no fear
A seasoned street fighter can smell fear just like a shark smells blood in the water. Being able to conquer your fear is a great tool to prevent empowering your opponent.

When intense fear consumes the body, you will begin to shake uncontrollably. This commonly occurs in the hands and legs. Your voice may crack, and you may stutter when you speak. Tunnel vision will set in, and you might not be able to focus or maintain eye contact. An assailant will quickly recognize these signs and become more emboldened hen they realize you are scared. Even when you are scared, don't let the opponent know it. Give the impression that you thrive under pressure. The previous exercises can help you control these reactions and reduce the probability that your attacker will capitalize on your fear.

Instilling fear and uncertainty in others
By contrast to the previous scenario, a high level of self confidence achieved by conquering your fear can cause a potential attacker to back down and have second thoughts about confronting you.

Using your trigger word to activate controlled aggression can also instill fear in an opponent. Take a moment and think about who you would rather fight, the reserved person who is saying they don't want any problems, or the raging mad man who is bouncing off the walls and drooling down his own chin? I'd rather deal with an angry dog over a rabid dog any day.

A word of caution about ignoring fear
There is a very fine line between courage and stupidity. Being able to stand up to your fears and conquer them does not mean you should take foolish chances or risks when unwarranted. Fear is not our enemy, but rather a natural reaction that helps protect us from harm. We must think of fear as a personal advisor that lets us know when there is danger ahead. Although we consider the advice, we make our own decisions and act accordingly. We are not controlled by the advisor. Use fear to your advantage and channel its power into your response but remember that you are the boss over your fear.

The Checkers Principle

Although I am familiar with the game of chess, I was always more of a checkers person. My grandfather and my great grandmother were both masters of the game. As a child, I would play checkers with my great grandmother and she would easily beat me. She was always several moves ahead of me and seemed to know what my next move would be before I made it. One of her favorite strategies was to lure me into a position where she had me no matter what move I made. Interestingly, the strategies used to win the game of checkers can also be applied to the martial arts.

In the early nineties, I began studying Brazilian Jiujitsu. I had a brown belt in Judo at the time, so I was very familiar with ground fighting, armlocks, and choking techniques. One major difference I immediately noticed between the two arts was that in Brazilian Jiujitsu, you are always thinking one or two steps ahead of your opponent. When the opponent was controlled on the ground, his options were limited which allowed you to have a specific response to whatever he may do next.

A clear example of this was the cross armbar or Juji-Gatame. I learned the cross armbar in Judo and could execute it very well. It was typically applied after taking the opponent to the ground with some type of throw, but I was never shown how to set up the lock or transition to it from other techniques. By contrast, in one of my first Brazilian Jiujitsu lessons, I was taught how to apply the cross armbar from the mount position if the opponent is pushing with his arms straight.

One of the major concepts that Brazilian Jiujitsu taught me was to control the opponent in order to limit his possible actions, then have your own finishing response for whatever action the opponent chooses to make. Once I understood this concept, I realized what a valuable tool it was, and I began to apply it to other areas of my martial arts study. Because I believe this concept is so important, we will break it down in more detail.

To better understand this concept in motion, let's look at the game of checkers one more time. There is a rule in checkers that you must jump the opponent's game piece if a jump is available. A common strategy is to sacrifice one checker by making the opponent take his jump, which then sets you up for multiple jumps of the opponent's game pieces. By forcing the opponent to take his jump, you are limiting his actions. When he responds with the action you know he will take, you are then prepared to finish him with multiple jumps of your own. You have essentially set him up and made him play your game. This concept can be broken down into the following steps.

Step One-Control the Opponent's Movement

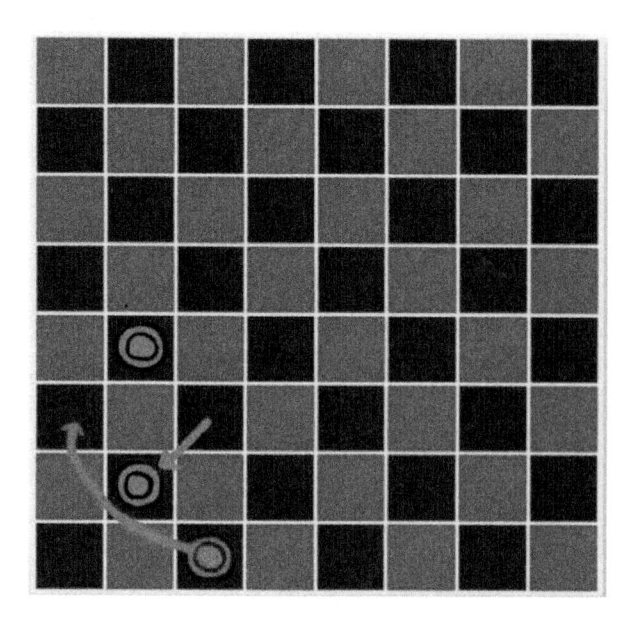

Understanding that the rules of checkers require an opponent to take a jump when present, you move your checker (black) to a position that forces the opponent's next move. By jumping your checker piece, the opponent unknowingly places himself in a position that is exactly where you wanted him to be.

Step Two- Limit the Opponent's Options

After the opponent completes his jump, you move your second checker piece to the black square straight across from him. This limits the opponent to only two possible moves. He can move his checker piece diagonally upward or diagonally downward. Either move he makes will put you in a position to finish the game.

Step Three- Finish Him

With the opponent's choices limited, he has to move his checker piece to one of the two diagonal spaces. Regardless of the space he chooses, you will jump his piece and win the game. Again, you were operating two moves ahead of him from the start.

Now we will look at the same principle again from a Jiujitsu perspective. Let's say you have taken the opponent to the ground and achieved the mount position. From this position the opponent's options are very limited. He might try to bump or push you off of him, roll to his stomach to protect his face, roll to his side, or do nothing at all.

Regardless of what he does, you have a response prepared to finish the fight. You are controlling the situation to limiting his actions, then responding appropriately to any action he chooses. Once again, you are a step ahead of him the entire time. Let's look at how this concept plays out.

From the mount position, your opponent has limited options available to him. You can strike at will, and it is very difficult for him to strike back at you because gravity and reach are working against him. His options can be summarized as follows.

Options Available to the opponent

1) He flails around and tries to bump or roll you off of him.
2) He tries to push you off of him with his arms.
3) He rolls to his side to try and protect himself against your strikes.
4) He rolls to his stomach to avoid punches to his face and tries to get up.
5) He does nothing (really not an option)

Your Response to Option One

You are mounted on the opponent and prepared to throw punches. The opponent tries desperately to bump or roll you off, you stabilize the position by using your body weight, hooking his legs, staying high on his chest, and controlling the head. The opponent eventually becomes tired and you can finish him with striking techniques or a submission.

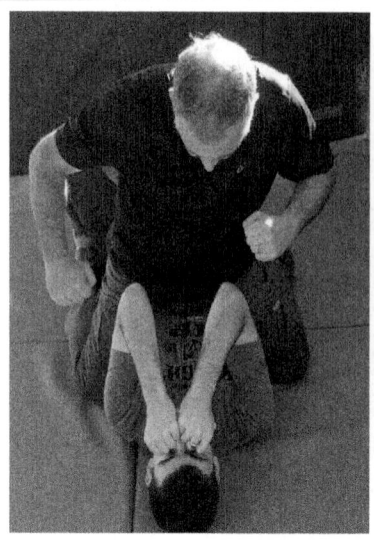

Your Response to Option Two

As you attack, the opponent tries to push you off of him. You trap one of his arms, put weight on his chest, and swing your leg over his head to apply a cross armbar that finishes the encounter.

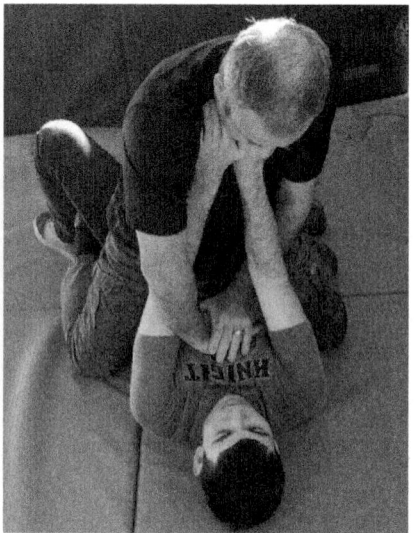

Forging The Mind And Body

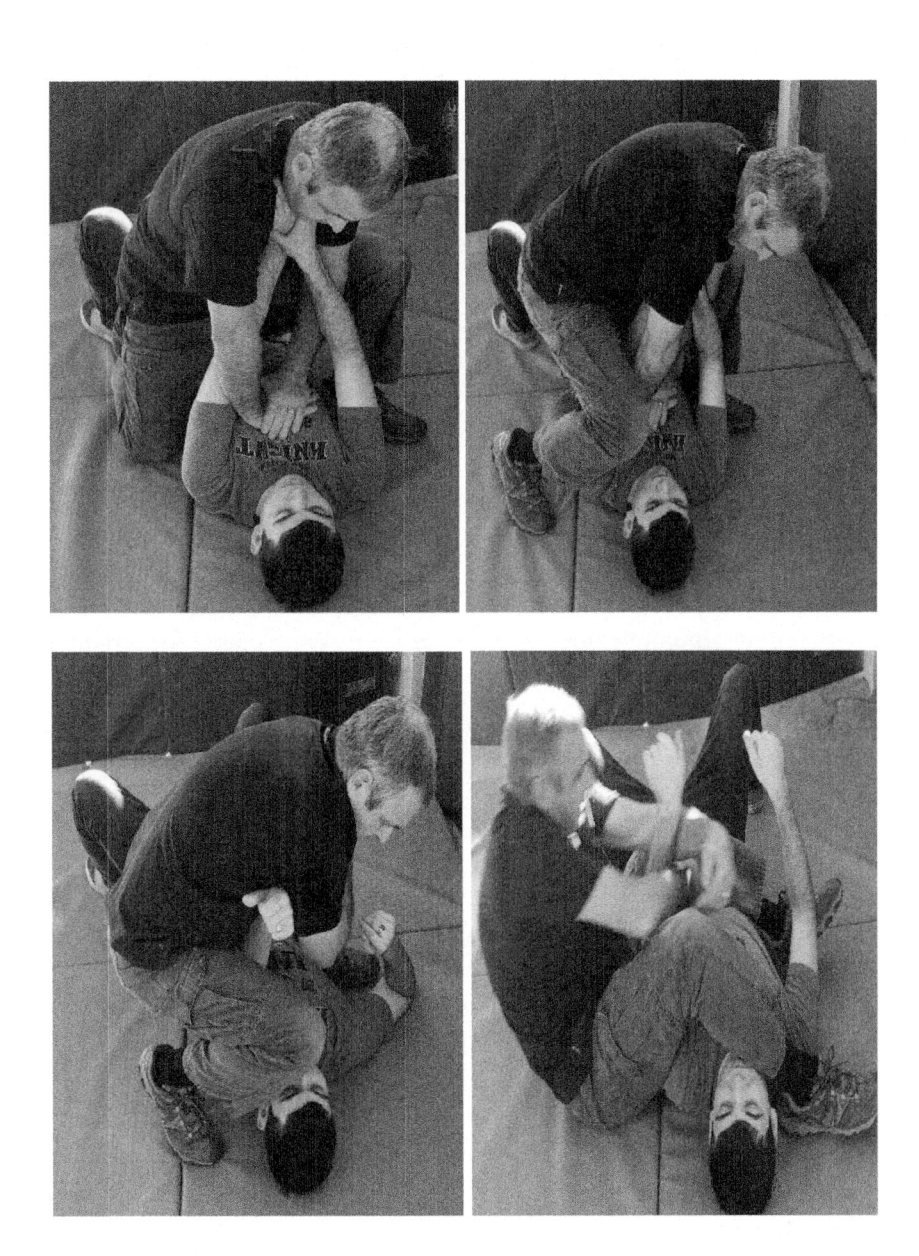

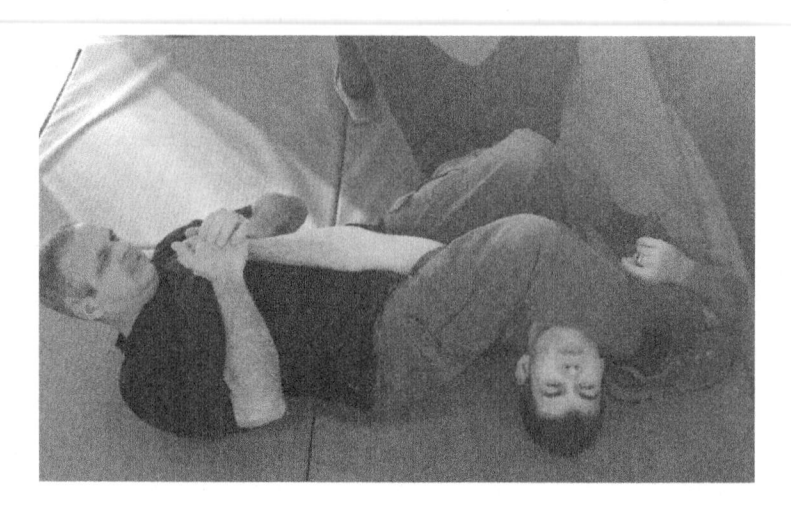

Your Response to Option Three

As you attack the opponent in the mount, he rolls to his side and tries to cover against your strikes. You shift to a side mount and push his elbow forward as you grasp his hand from under his head. From this position, the opponent is helpless to your punches. You could also apply a choke or an armbar to finish him from here.

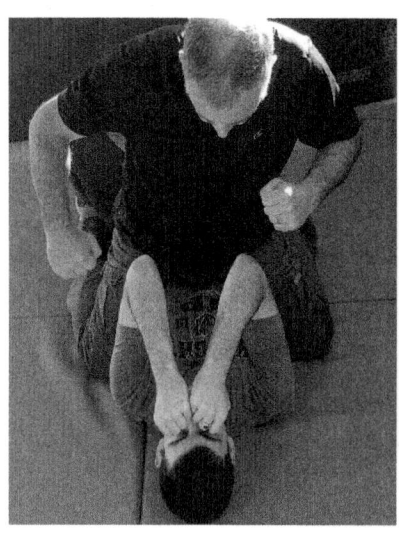

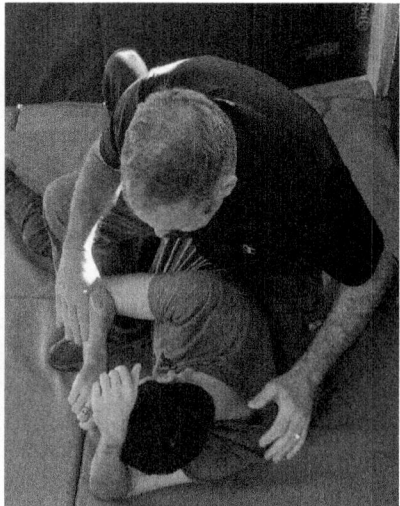

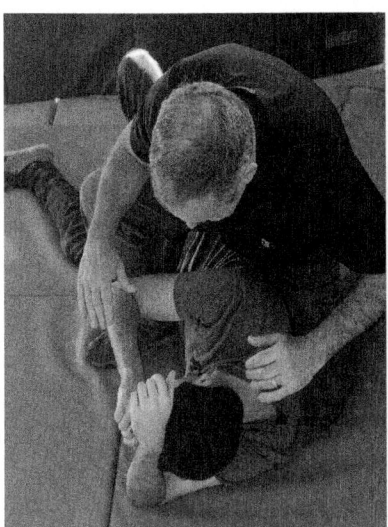

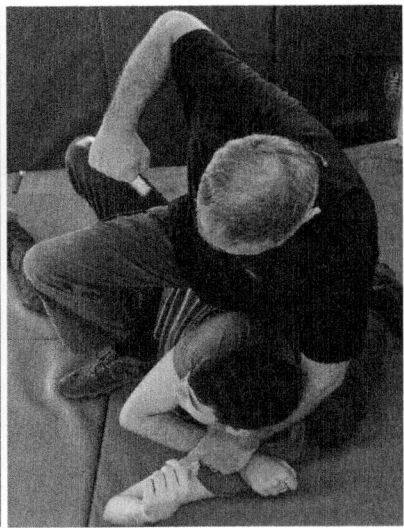

Your Response to Option Four

As you strike the opponent from the mount position, he rolls to his stomach to avoid the anslaught of punches. You continue to strike the back of his neck with elbows. When the opponent goes to his knees and tries to stand up, you put your hooks in and control his upperbody. From this position the opponent continues to struggle and rolls to his back. You apply a rear naked choke to finish him off.

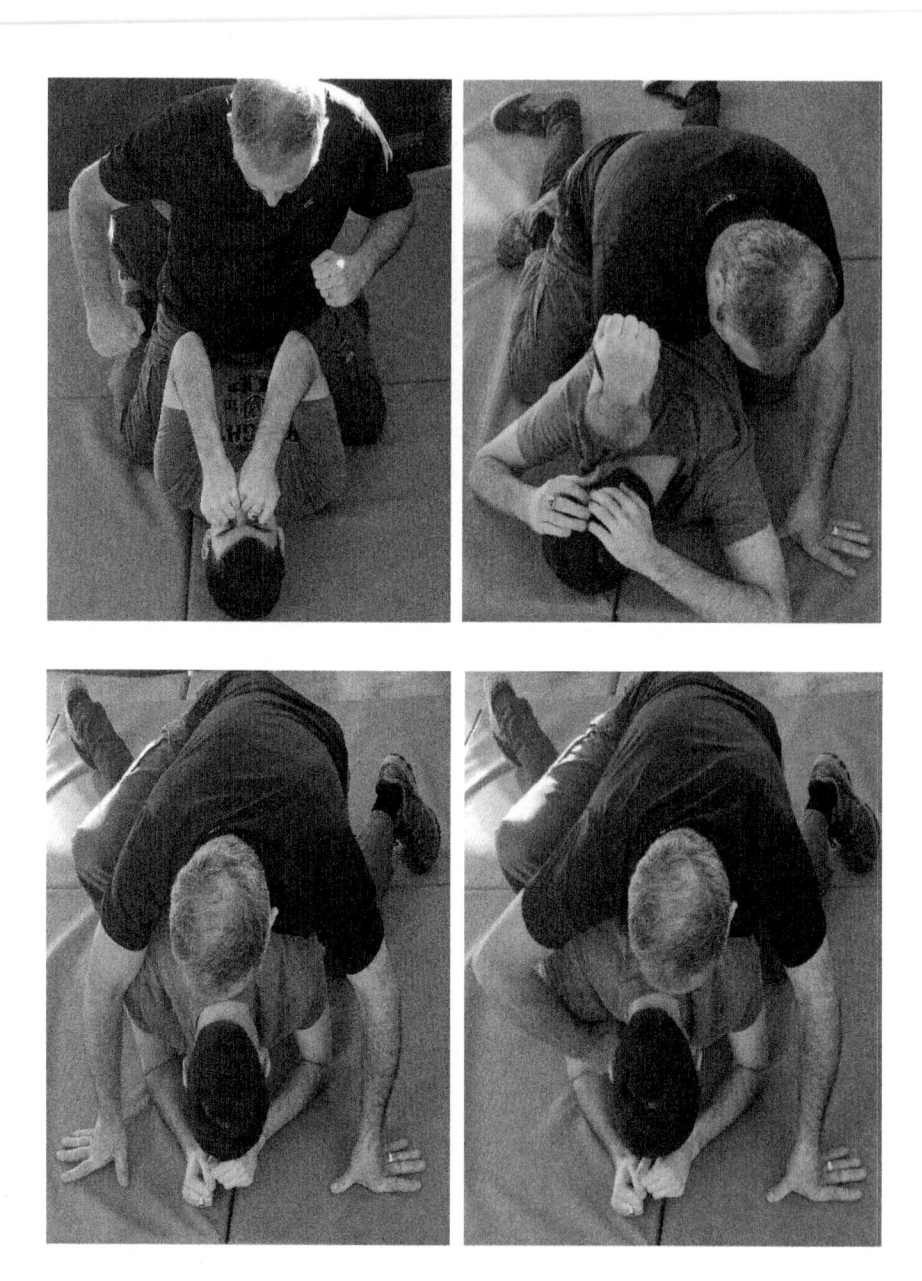

Forging The Mind And Body

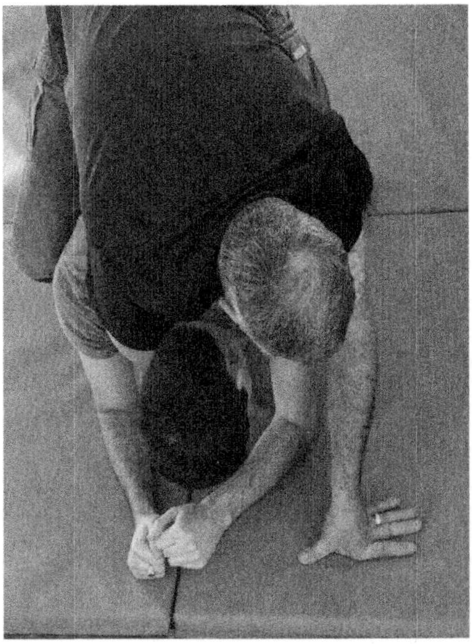

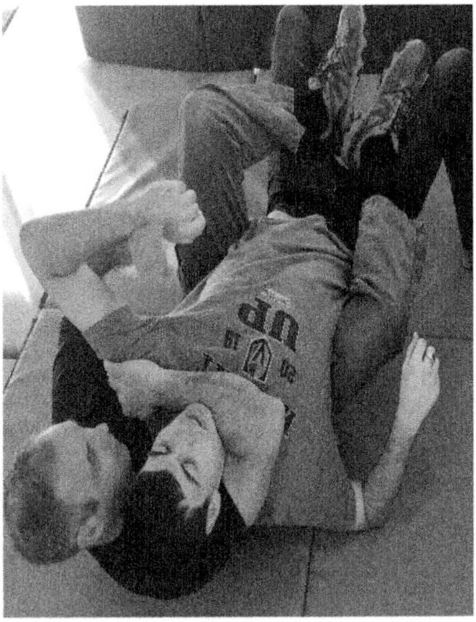

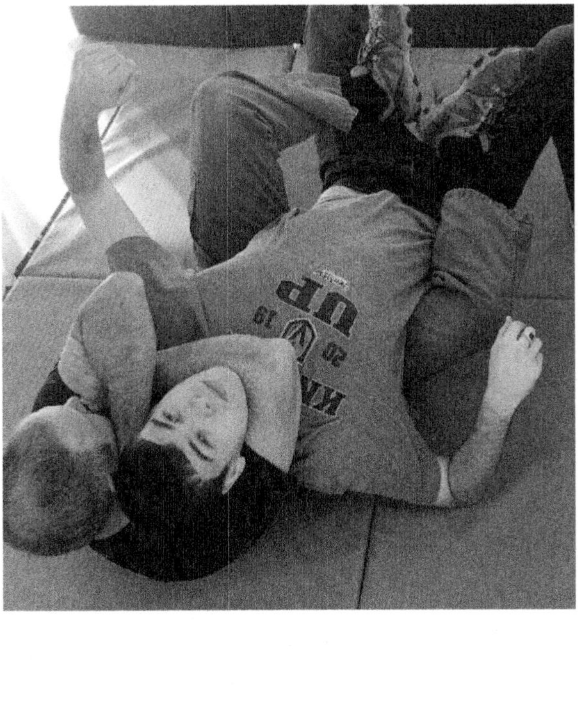

Your Response to Option Five

If the opponent chooses to do nothing, you are in control and can decide the amount of force that you need to use to end the situation. There is really no reason for the opponent to do nothing unless he has given up, is unconscious, or too exhausted to fight back.

As you can see, just like the game of checkers, you control the opponent, limit his options, and have a response for any option he chooses. He plays your game instead of you playing his. You are probably asking how this concept can be applied beyond Jiujitsu. We will now discuss methods to incorporate the checkers concept into all aspects of your martial arts.

In the striking game, it becomes much more difficult to limit your opponent's options than in the grappling game. First, the opponent is mobile, and second, he has a wide range of weapons available to use such as kicks, punches, elbows, and knee strikes. The opponent also has a greater possibility of using improvised weapons and the environment to his advantage. The ability to control the opponent on the ground negates many of these factors that become difficult to control when standing.

Even if you can limit the opponent's options, you must have your own response plan to whatever attack he chooses, and this plan must be able to end the fight. For example, a parry is a nice response to a striking attack, but it doesn't end the fight. By using a strategy that includes the following elements, you can begin to effectively employ the checkers principle in your stand-up game.

Checkers principle for stand-up and weapons fighting

1) Zone to limit the opponent's weapon options.
2) Reduce the opponent's mobility.

3) Use the environment to your advantage.
4) Set the opponent up.
5) Use a finishing technique to end the encounter.

Zone to limit the opponent's weapon options
Zoning is the term used to describe the action of moving in and to the side of your opponent. By doing this, you place yourself in a position of advantage at the opponent's side where he can no longer strike you with both hands and feet without turning to face you again.

To test this concept, stand facing your training partner. You will immediately notice that he can strike you with both of his hands, both of his feet, both knees, both elbows, and his head. He basically has nine weapons available to use against you. Now step forward and to the right side at a forty-five-degree angle. You will now be standing on your partner's left side. Notice how from this position he is very limited in his ability to attack you. He could strike out sideways with his hand or elbow, or side kick with his leg, but unless he takes the time to turn towards you again, you have negated over half of his weapons.

In addition to limiting the opponent's weapons, zoning negates the power in his strikes. When you stand directly in front of your attacker, you face the full power of his attacks, but when you use the zoning principle, you move away from the area where the attack would generate the most power.

Reduce the opponent's mobility
When ground fighting, you have the ability to limit the opponent's mobility by controlling his body with a position such as a scarf hold, the guard, or mount. This becomes much more difficult when standing. The three primary methods for limiting your opponent's

mobility are, grabbing him, stepping on his foot, and pinning him against an object.

Grabbing the opponent can include gripping his clothing, holding a limb, or clinching. Stepping on his foot as you enter can limit his ability to retreat or move laterally. Pinning the opponent can be done against a wall, a vehicle, fire hydrant, park bench, or any number of obstacles you might encounter on the street.

Use the environment to your advantage

We have already touched on this concept by discussing how you can pin your opponent against various objects, but the environment can also be used to assist you in other ways. For example, moving to a position where the sun is in your opponent's eyes will limit his ability to see and respond to your attacks. Forcing an opponent who is a good kicker into a confined area can limit his ability to use his kicking skills against you. You should always be scanning your surroundings to identify potential dangers to avoid, and how you can use the environment to help you achieve your goals.

Set the opponent up

There are many ways you can set your opponent up and get him to react in a way that can be used to your advantage. One of the most common methods is called drawing. Drawing is basically leaving an opening in your defense that tempts the opponent to attack. When he strikes the perceived opening, you respond with a pre-planned counterattack.

Another way to set up your opponent is to execute a strike to elicit a desired reaction. This can be as simple as throwing a groin kick to cause the opponent to bend forward, then striking the eyes, or grabbing the neck to clinch. Off balancing the opponent can also be used as a set up technique. When a person tries to regain their balance, it is a normal reaction for them to use their hands to brace against an object to try and stop their fall. This gives you the opportunity to grab their bracing limb and execute techniques such as joint locks or takedowns.

Through constant sparring and practice with your training partner, you can experiment with setting up different attacks and luring him into your trap. Be sure to apply this concept to all aspects of your training to gain the best benefit.

Use a finishing technique to end the encounter

This may sound like common sense, but you would be surprised how often people train to fight with no real plan of attack for finishing the opponent and ending the encounter quickly. You should analyze the techniques you practice seeing which of those techniques are effective for finishing a fight. Techniques such as choke holds, power punches, joint attacks, and strikes to vital areas such as the throat, groin, knees, and eyes, all have a much better chance of ending an encounter than a simple punch or kick. Obviously, it makes no sense to limit the opponent's weapons, reduce his mobility, set him up, and then not have a plan to finish him off. This would be like standing in line for hours at the bank with no money to deposit.

The following series of photographs shows one example of how the checkers principle can be used in a standing encounter. As the attacker starts to throw a rear punch, the defender zones in on a forty-five-degree angle to the right. From this position, the attacker's ability to use all of his weapons to strike is limited. The defender then aggressively shoves the attacker into the wall to limit his mobility. He uses the environment to his advantage by pinning the attacker against the wall immediately following the shove. As the attacker braces with his arms to push back away from the wall, the defender uses an elbow strike to his arm to injure the elbow joint and set the arm up for a grab. With the attacker's arm secured, the defender applies an arm bar to break the attacker's arm and finish the fight.

Forging The Mind And Body

Controlling the Ego

As we go about our life it is easy to get caught up in all of the daily hustle and bustle. We sometimes get frustrated while driving or get offended when others infringe upon our personal space. Many people hold their frustration inside and then one small thing will cause all of those bent up emotions to come rushing to the surface. This is when controlling your ego can be critical.

I remember many years ago driving with some family members to my brother's house. My aunt, uncle and parents had all come to visit from out of town, and I had rented a van so I could get them around easier. I had worked all day, was tired, and had hit some heavy traffic so I was not in the best of moods.

As we approached my brother's neighborhood, there was a bicyclist riding slowly in the center of the road. I followed behind him for a minute at a snail's pace, and several times he looked back over his shoulder and made eye contact, but he refused to move over so that myself and other cars could get by. It soon became obvious that his actions were intentional when he started to weave from side to side in the roadway.

The bike rider was a rough looking guy, in fact, my initial impression was that he probably just got out of prison and was selling drugs in the neighborhood. Finally, my patience was at its end, and I accelerated the van around him. As I passed him, I honked the horn and gave him a stare. I saw him flip me off in the rear-view mirror as I turned onto my brother's street. In my mind the incident was over, but unfortunately it had just begun.

I parked the van in front of my brother's house and got out to open the side door so my family could get out. That's when I looked up and saw the bike rider peddling aggressively in my direction. When he got about twenty feet from me, he jumped off of the bicycle and threw it down in the street. He then came straight up to me with his hands clenched yelling at the top of his lungs.

I was initially caught off guard and took a step backwards to create distance. I raised my hands up above my waist and angled my body slightly to protect myself should he decide to attack. Instead, he began screaming, "you got a problem mother f-er?" He then proceeded to describe in great detail the many horrible things he was about to do to me. At this point, I could have de-escalated the situation, and acted like a rational person, but I didn't. Instead, I let my ego take control and responded with some choice words of my own.

I had already made up my mind that a fight was about to occur, and I was planning my attack. I would blast this guy with kicks and punches, clinch, take him to the ground, and finish him with JiujItsu. As my plan of attack unfolded in my mind, I noticed a decent sized knife clipped in his belt. At that point it became obvious that if I started to get the best of this guy, that knife would no doubt come into play.

The guy continued to yell and move closer towards me to get in my face. I stepped backwards to maintain distance which he seemed to take as a sign of fear. The moment I stepped back, he became more aggressive and I knew the fight was about to happen any second. That's when I tried a different strategy.

I made a gesture towards the knife that was clipped on his belt and said, "I see you have a knife, well I've got a gun". The guy instantly started to scan me with his eyes to determine if I was carrying a firearm. He slowly backed up and picked up his bicycle. "F--- you!" he said. "Your not worth going back to prison for". Then he got on the bike and rode off. I turned towards the van and saw my relatives watching all of this unfold with wide eyes. Later I found out that my uncle tried to get out of the van to help me, but my aunt told him I had it under control and wouldn't let him.

Luckily, this situation ended without violence, but the fact is it never should have happened in the first place. I could have easily gone around the bicyclist when the opportunity presented itself. I didn't have to honk my horn at him or make comments. I was already tired and frustrated from work and traffic, and I let those emotions surface. I made many mistakes that day, but my ego was the primary force that fueled the fire.

Of all things that can get you into trouble quickly, I believe that ego is at the top of the list. Among the top reasons why murders and violent assaults occur in our country are drugs, robbery, gangs, and disrespect. When we feel like we have been disrespected, or infringed upon, our egos can't let that go without setting the violator straight. At times we see this occur just by someone allegedly looking at another person funny. When we learn to control our ego and eliminate the inner desire to hold others accountable for treading on us, we can prevent about ninety percent of the physical confrontations we might encounter.

One of the best ways to control your ego and reduce your desire to lash back at others when they wrong you, is to increase your martial arts skills. Training and skill development will give you added self-confidence. When you are extremely confident in your abilities, you no longer feel the need to prove yourself to others. When you have nothing to prove, your ego is a lot easier to control. In fact, it will become almost nonexistent.

There is a direct correlation between self-confidence and ego. When one goes up, the other goes down. Typically, the people who run their mouths the most, or try to prove how tough they are, actually have the least amount of self-confidence. By contrast, the person with the most self confidence is usually very reserved, polite, and not easily angered. The interesting thing is that when both self-confidence and ego are on the same level, you can hardly tell the difference between the two.

Ego Exercise One
Deflection

To perform the deflection exercise, decide that you will spend a day deflecting any perceived insults, infringements, or challenges to your pride. Imagine that you are wearing an invisible suit of armor that protects you from any negativity that comes your way. When someone cuts in front of you in line, swerves into your lane of traffic, or looks at you funny, just smile back at them as their actions are deflected by your armor.

Your invisible armor doesn't allow any insults or negativity to penetrate and irritate you. Because nothing sinks in, there is no reason to be offended by anything someone does. There is no reason to hold anyone accountable for their actions. Throughout the day, try to forgive anyone who treads on you even in the slightest way. Continue to smile and let it all bounce off of your protective armor.

Luckily, as we grow older, we have an opportunity to learn from our mistakes of youth. In contrast to the previous story I told, I recently had another altercation that started in a similar manner.

I was driving home from a shopping center when a car suddenly swerved over in front of me, barely missing my bumper. I instinctively hit my brakes and honked my horn at the aggressive motorist who had just cut me off and almost caused an accident. A short distance later, I stopped for a traffic light and I noticed that the car that cut me off was pulled up along side of me with the window down.

My window was also down due to the nice weather and I could hear the driver yelling at me. I glanced over and he began yelling at me again, angry because I had honked my horn at him. I could feel my blood starting to boil inside of me. I couldn't believe the audacity of this guy who almost hit me with his car, now yelling at me because I honked at him. I was angry and wanted to lash out at this idiot.

This time, I kept my emotions in check and did not let my ego take control of the situation. Instead of yelling back at him, I simply smiled and said, "No one got hurt, it's all good!" I saw the expression on the aggressive driver's face change immediately from a look of anger to a look of surprise. It was if the wind was immediately taken out of his sails. The light changed to green and I drove away with no further issues from the other vehicle.

Controlling our egos takes a lot of effort. It isn't an easy process, but over time we can learn to keep it in check. By training hard in our chosen martial arts systems, increasing our skills and building self-confidence, we can suppress the ego and avoid the many negative consequences that arise from having an ego which is unchecked.

Psychological Strategy

One of the most powerful weapons you have at your disposal is the ability to influence the mind and actions of your opponent. Phycological strategy and the martial arts have gone hand in hand since the beginning of time. For centuries, martial artists have used psychological strategy to fool and intimidate their enemies.

Imagine for a moment that you are an ancient warrior preparing for battle. Hours before the battle is to occur, a scout returns from a reconnaissance of the enemy. The scout has troubling news to report. Even though your troops out number the enemy fighters three to one, it appears that they are protected by some type of powerful force.

The scout proceeds to describe how he has witnessed the enemy fighters catching arrows with their bare hands, resisting fire, taking sword strikes to their bodies without being cut, and killing enemy prisoners with just a touch. These enemy warriors obviously possess some paranormal skills that will make them almost impossible for your forces to defeat. What would your mind set be going into this battle? After hearing the stories from the scout, many of your troops desert the battlefield and the general decides not to engage the enemy.

The reality is that the enemy warriors did not possess any extraordinary skills, but they were masters of psychological strategy. Knowing that their actions were under observation from the scout, they used trickery to their advantage. They struck each other with dull training swords after cleverly switching them with the actual sharp ones. They practiced catching training arrows, walking on hot coals, and striking prisoners who had already been poisoned. It was nothing more than magic tricks and sleight of hand, but it helped them avoid a battle they otherwise couldn't have won.

I believe that many of the esoteric practices associated with the martial arts today have their roots in psychological strategy. Take for example the traditional belief in some styles that a weapon is endowed with a spirit of its own that can protect the user or in some case turn against the user if not treated with proper respect. I have heard stories regarding the sword known as the kris which is commonly used in the Indonesian art of Pencak Silat.

It was traditionally believed that the kris was possessed by a spirit. This spirit could cause the sword to jump from its scabbard at will and greatly enhance the skill level of anyone who wields it. It was also believed that once drawn from the scabbard, it must taste blood before it is sheathed or the spirit in the blade will become angry and turn on the owner. I have witnessed Silat practitioners demonstrate a technique involving an almost imperceivable jerk of the wrist that propels the kris upwards and out of its scabbard. When perfected, this technique would make it appear as though the sword magically leaps from the sheath on its own.

Psychological strategies of this nature actually serve a dual purpose. First, they strike fear and apprehension into the hearts and minds of adversaries. Second, they instill confidence and determination in the fighter. It would obviously be intimidating to believe that your opponent is in possession of a magical sword that can leap from its sheath to attack you on its own. But also imagine the power a tribal leader could harness, if he presented you with a blade and told you it was possessed by the spirit of a fallen warrior. If you fail to quench the blade's thirst for blood when battle occurs, it will become angry and turn against you. You would probably fight a little harder when the time came for battle.

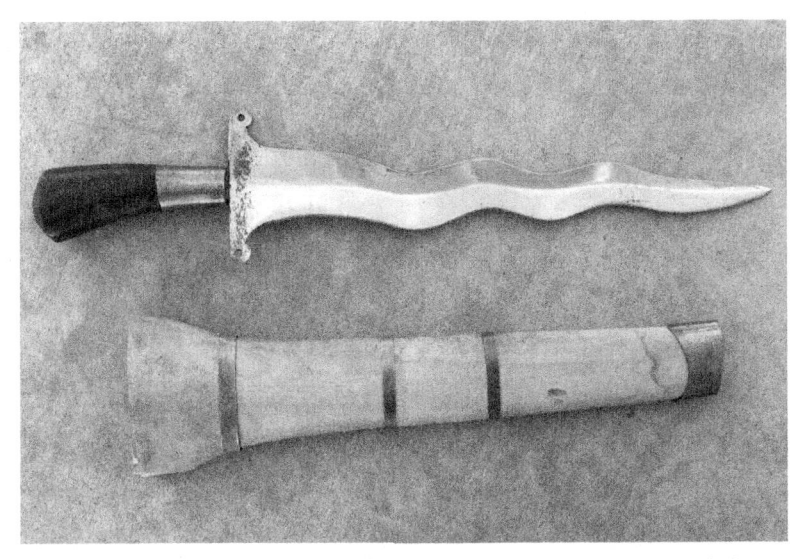

The kris sword was thought to possess a spirit

How can we use psychological strategies to our advantage today? Are there ways to employ some of these concepts into our martial arts training so that we can use them when a real encounter occurs? The answer is yes! Below are a few examples of how psychological strategies can be used to trick, intimidate, or influence an opponent so they are less likely to physically engage you. It should be known that some of these strategies could backfire and have the opposite effect if taken too far or overused.

Feigning an altered state or condition

The idea of pretending to be impaired or disabled has been used as a psychological strategy for centuries. There are entire Kung-Fu systems based on imitating the movements of drunks. If an opponent thinks you are a harmless drunk, they might drop their guard and not perceive you as a threat until it is too late.

Most people in in a civilized society would be less likely to attack someone who they believe is disabled or injured. If they happen to be one of the evil individuals who would attack someone who is injured or disabled, their guard will probably be down, and they will not believe you can cause them any harm.

Pretending to be under the influence of drugs, or just downright crazy can also intimidate a would-be attacker and convince them to leave you alone. After all, who wants to fight a crazy person that has no concern for their own wellbeing. Yelling random things that make no sense, erratic body movements, pulling your hair, and aggressively scratching yourself can all give the impression that you are in some type of a mental health crisis and it might not be in the attacker's best interest to mess with you.

In very rare cases, pretending to be dead or unconscious might be a survival option. We have all heard the horrific stories where someone lay still during a shooting rampage and the attacker passed them by believing they were dead. Obviously, this type of strategy is extremely risky and should only be used as a last resort when escape or fighting is not a viable option.

Convincing the opponent that you are not alone

I remember studying the Civil War in school and learning about the Confederate general who was significantly outnumbered by Union troops. He marched the few soldiers he had through an opening in the woods where the enemy could see. Once out of sight, the troops would circle back around and march through the same opening again. This gave the illusion that the general had an endless amount of troops at his disposal, which caused the Union army to rethink their attack. There is strength in numbers.

Convincing a possible assailant that you have friends nearby who are coming to assist you, can be a useful strategy. This could be accomplished by pretending to be on your cell phone or by yelling out to the park across the street as if you are talking to a group of your friends there. If you are being followed, walking up to a group of strangers, and acting like you know them could cause the assailant to leave you alone.

This strategy is also commonly employed by street gangs. You will probably not start a fight with a person who is part of an outlaw motorcycle club, if you know you will have to deal with the entire gang down the road. Convincing someone that you are a member of an elite organization, or a group that will not take kindly to someone messing with one of their members, could be a successful strategy to use.

The strategy of being gross and disgusting

It is a fact that people usually do not want anything to do with someone that is doing something disgusting or gross. I know it sounds crazy, but picking your nose, slobbering down your chin, digging ear wax from your ear, urinating on yourself, or vomiting might cause a would-be aggressor to leave you alone. After all, if you are vomiting, maybe you are sick and will contaminate them with what ever disease you are carrying. At the very least, people usually don't want to get your snot or urine on them.

This psychological strategy can also involve the use of blood to persuade someone to leave you alone. In today's day and age, most people are well aware of blood borne pathogens. Biting the inside of your lip will produce blood that you could allow to run down your mouth and chin. If you have suffered a minor injury, and are bleeding, showing no concern for your own welfare, and flailing your own blood around plays into the previous strategy of making the attacker believe you are crazy. Although these examples may seem very extreme, if you find yourself in a life-or-death situation, anything you can do to survive the encounter would be welcome.

The secret knowledge or hidden weapons

Another common psychological strategy that has been used for centuries is to convince others that you possess a hidden weapon or secret knowledge that gives you the advantage over them. As a kid growing up in the seventies, the martial arts were still relatively unknown by most people. The movies and television portrayed martial artists as deadly fighters who could kill with a single blow. The urban legend spread quickly that black belts had to register their hands as deadly weapons.

During this time, merely assuming a Karate stance at the start of a situation would often persuade an aggressor to move on and avoid conflict. I knew people that had no martial arts knowledge, who assumed a Karate type stance when confronted and it actually worked. Obviously, times have changed, and this would probably not work as well today, but the basic strategy can still be used. Bouncing on your feet like a boxer or moving in a position similar to a wrestler might convince a would-be attacker that you are a seasoned fighter and accomplish the same goal that assuming the Karate stance once did.

In addition to convincing the opponent that you have a secret physical skill, you can also simulate the possession of a weapon. Reaching into a coat pocket, your waistline, or under a jacket with one of your hands, can convince someone that you have a weapon, even if you don't. Concealing one hand behind your back, or down at your side also serves the same purpose. Again, all of these strategies must be used cautiously when no other options are available. In some cases they might only escalate the situation rather than having the desired goal. No strategy is effective in all situations but having knowledge of these skills will improve your chances of surviving when a deadly encounter occurs.

In this chapter we have only scratched the surface of

psychological strategies. Entire books could be written on this subject alone. I encourage you to study the vast amount of information that is available today on this subject and consider how these principles can be used to enhance your fighting skills.

Resistance

Resistance is a concept that unfortunately is missing in many martial arts schools today. The vast majority of students are taught fighting techniques and they practice them with a cooperative training partner who offers little to no resistance. When they eventually spar with other students, all of the technique they have learned go out the window and they resort to exchanging blows. When they do attempt one of the techniques they have been taught against a resisting opponent, they fail, and they begin to believe the techniques don't work.

The sad thing is that many of these students never go beyond this level in the art they chose to study. They either quit completely or switch to another system that has a reputation for effectiveness. This process can actually poison an entire martial arts style and eventually lead people to believe the traditional martial arts are ineffective and useless.

In order to have confidence that your skills will work for you in a real encounter, you must train with resistance. This doesn't mean that you learn a technique today and then try it in sparring, it means you must incorporate increased levels of resistance until you are able to effectively apply the technique against someone who doesn't want you to pull it off. To show how you can easily incorporate resistance levels into your training, we will look at the example of a simple inside wrist lock. Although we will be examining the process with an inside wrist lock technique, the following examples show the stages of resistance that should be used to develop every technique you learn.

Stage One-No Resistance

In the first stage of training, you learn the mechanics of the inside wrist lock. Your training partner acts as a dummy and simply puts out his arm so you can learn how the technique is applied. At this stage, your partner helps you by telling you if the technique feels correct and is properly locking the joint. He also provides feedback about your body position, where you may be vulnerable to counter attacks, and goes with the momentum of the technique. As you apply the technique in this stage, your training partner takes the fall for you and break falls or rolls when the move is successfully completed.

As your skills increase at this level, you pick up the speed, but there is still no resistance from your partner. Eventually you can throw your cooperative training partner around the mat with ease and he jumps right back up to do it again. For someone watching you perform the technique at this stage, you appear to be very skilled.

Unfortunately, many martial artists never go beyond this stage because they believe they have mastered the technique and they have a false sense of confidence. If they ever have the unfortunate circumstance occur where they attempt the wrist lock under real conditions, they will most likely fail. Everything they have trained for falls apart and they lose confidence in their art and themselves.

Stage Two-Mild Resistance

Once you have achieved a level of skill executing the technique with no resistance, you will have your training partner dial it up a notch. As you attempt the inside wrist lock, your training partner will move his hand slowly to try and prevent you from grabbing his wrist.

Once you secure the wrist, your partner will offer mild

resistance by tensing his arm and using muscle strength to resist the lock. Despite the mild resistance, your partner is still working to helping you master the technique. When he feels like you have the technique locked in, he will ease up on the resistance and allow you to complete the move. The resistance comes in the initial phase of application and is mild.

Stage Three-Moderate Resistance

At this stage, your training partner is trying to trip you up and prevent you from applying the technique at a moderate level. When you attempt to seize the opponent's wrist, he moves his hand quickly to avoid your grab. You are forced to immobilize him, use distraction techniques, and set up your partner in order to successfully capture his limb.

As you apply the wrist lock, your training partner resists with moderate force by tensing his arm, moving his body, and using muscular strength. When he feels the lock sinking in, he will comply. This is also the stage where your partner can use light counterstrikes if there is an opening in your defense. You will practice defending against any strikes from the opponent as you apply the wrist lock.

At this stage you may also begin to experiment with flowing into alternate locking techniques depending on the resistance your partner gives you. In cases where you fail to apply the wrist lock, transition into a striking technique, or disengage. If you are consistently failing at this stage, slow down and reduce the resistance slightly until your skills improve.

Stage Four-Full Resistance

When you reach the level where you can consistently apply the technique on your training partner with moderate resistance, it is time to move to the last stage where your training partner fully resists your attack.

At this stage you will attempt to apply your skills in contact sparring sessions. As you spar with your partner, you will find that although it is much more difficult to execute your techniques against an adversary who is fully resisting, you will have the advantage of surprise at this level because your partner will not know which technique to expect.

In some cases, techniques will actually work better against an opponent who is fully committed to causing you harm than against someone who is only partially resisting. This is especially true for techniques that involve off balancing and redirecting the opponent.

You are also free to flow from one technique to another at this level and respond to the actions of your partner. Your ability to adapt to the energy and movement of your training partner will be critical. When you can consistently apply your techniques under these conditions, you will have the confidence that your skills will not fail you in a real encounter.

Beyond Stage Four

You can take your level of skill beyond stage four by changing the dynamics and environment of your training. For example, you might spar against more than one training partner, or against a partner who is armed with a practice weapon. You might test your skills while waist deep in water, out in a dust storm, in a concrete alleyway, or in the snow. The sky is the limit and only you can decide how far you want to develop your skills, but at the bare minimum you must train your techniques to at least the level of stage four. The below photos show the progression of each stage of training for the inside wrist lock technique.

The Inside Wrist Lock-Stage One-No Resistance

At this stage, the practitioner is learning and perfecting the basic movements of the inside wrist lock with no resistance. He reaches across and grabs the fleshy part of the training partner's hand on the ring finger side. He then rotates his hand clockwise to point the training partner's fingers towards the sky. To complete the wrist lock, the practitioner pulls the training partner's hand close to his chest and applies forward pressure against his wrist joint. Throughout the training session, the partner provides feedback on how the technique was applied and if it was done properly. The practitioner continues to practice and improve until the lock can be applied flawlessly. This is the most common stage that many martial artists practice in and never move beyond.

The Inside Wrist Lock-Stage Two-Mild Resistance

Now the training partner dials it up a notch. As the practitioner attempts to grasp his hand, the training partner moves it away at a slow to moderate speed to avoid the grab. When the practitioner succeeds in grabbing the hand, he starts to apply the inside wrist lock, but the training partner resists by tensing his arm, bending it at the elbow, and using mild muscle strength. Once the practitioner is able to secure the lock, the training partner stops resisting. Remember that even at this stage, the training partner is working with the practitioner to help him learn the technique. He should provide advice on how the technique is being applied and correct any errors he notices. It should be mentioned that once you reach stage two and resistance is being used, caution should also be used. Never try to force a technique on your training partner or go beyond the point where injury might occur. If the Training partner taps, release the hold, or lock immediately. Always train with safety in mind.

Forging The Mind And Body

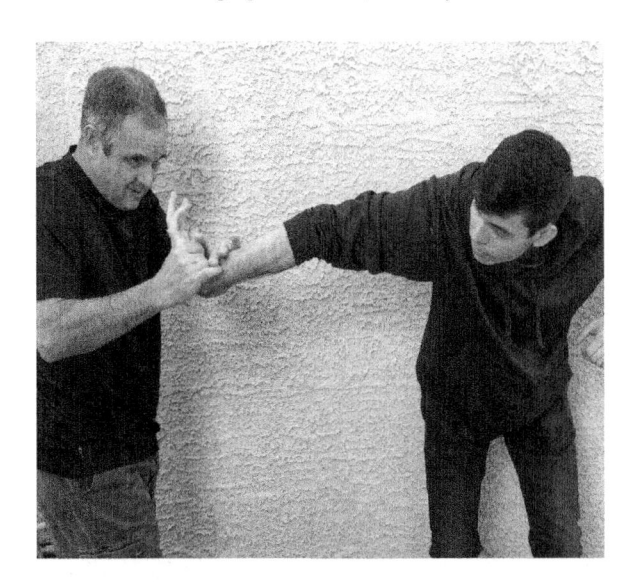

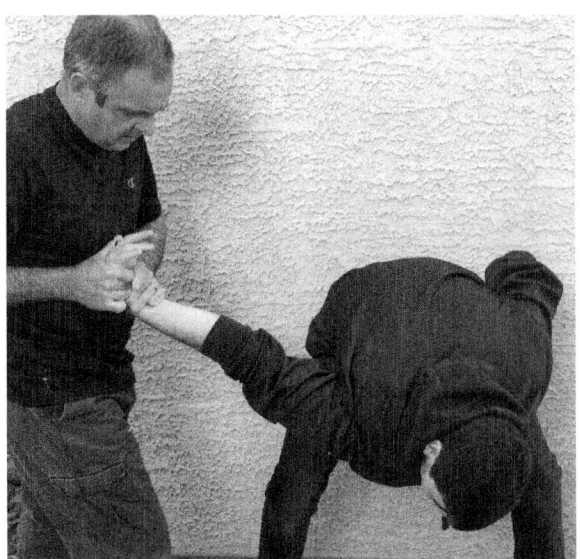

Inside Wrist Lock-Stage Three-Moderate Resistance

At stage three, the training partner increases his level of resistance to a moderate pace. The practitioner is now forced to get more aggressive. He steps on the training partner's foot as he moves in and launches an attack to set up the grab. The training partner moves his hand quicker to avoid capture, and once his wrist is secured, he uses more muscular strength to resist and prevent the lock from being applied. The training partner then throws a light punch to the practitioner's head while both of his hands are grasping his wrist. This requires the practitioner to release his grip with one hand in order to counter the punch with an outside parry. After successfully defending against the punch, he secures the wrist lock and gains control of the training partner. Keep in mind that while moderate resistance is being used, you are not sparring or fighting during this stage. The goal is to learn how to apply the technique under a moderate level of stress and resistance, but keep the training controlled and don't let it become a brawl.

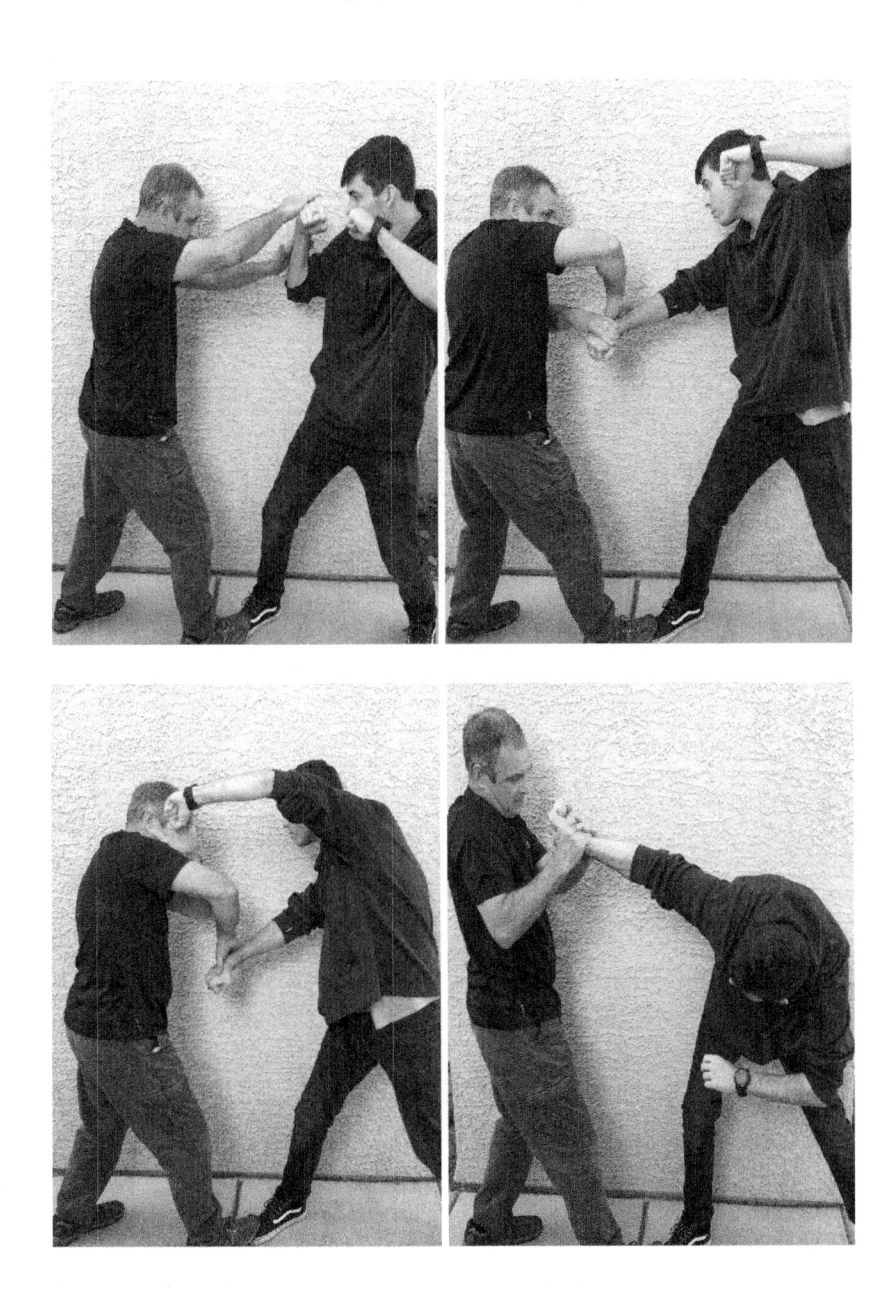

Forging The Mind And Body

Inside Wrist Lock-Stage Four-Full Resistance

At stage four, you are essentially sparring with your training partner and testing your techniques with full resistance. Before you progress to this stage, you should have the mechanics of the technique mastered and be able to pull it off regularly in practice against an opponent who provides moderate resistance. To be successful at this stage you must be able to adapt, move quickly, and control your opponent's mobility.

As the practitioner squares off with his sparring partner, the partner throws a lead punch. The practitioner simultaneously zones, parries, and counter punches. He then flows into a neck strike to distract his sparring partner as he catches his lead wrist. Next, the practitioner applies an inside wrist lock and starts to front kick the sparring partner's head, but he manages to resist the wrist lock by muscling upwards and bending his elbow. The practitioner realizes he is about to lose control of the wrist lock and flows into a shoulder lock and knee strike to end the encounter.

Forging The Mind And Body

Forging The Mind And Body

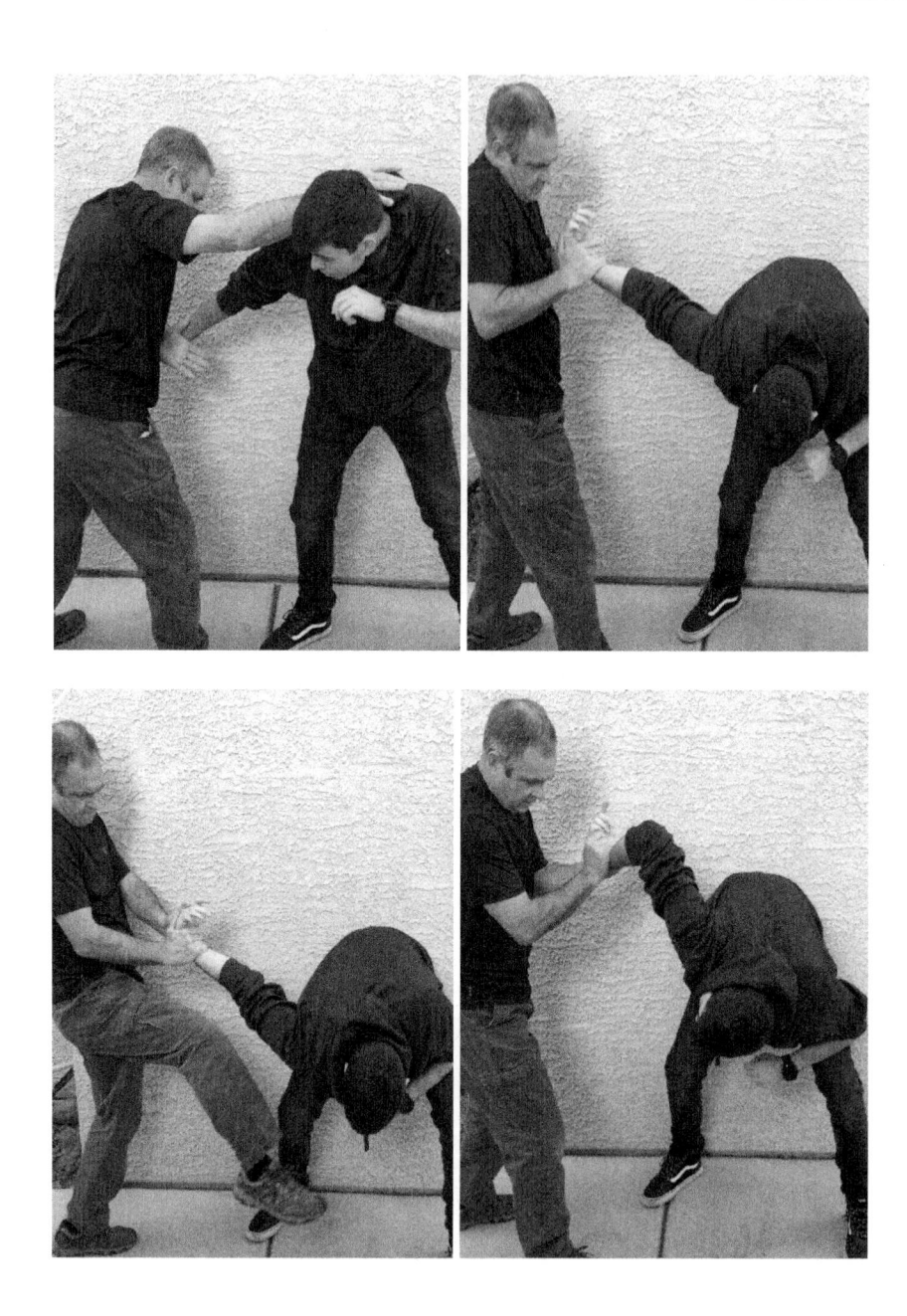

Forging The Mind And Body

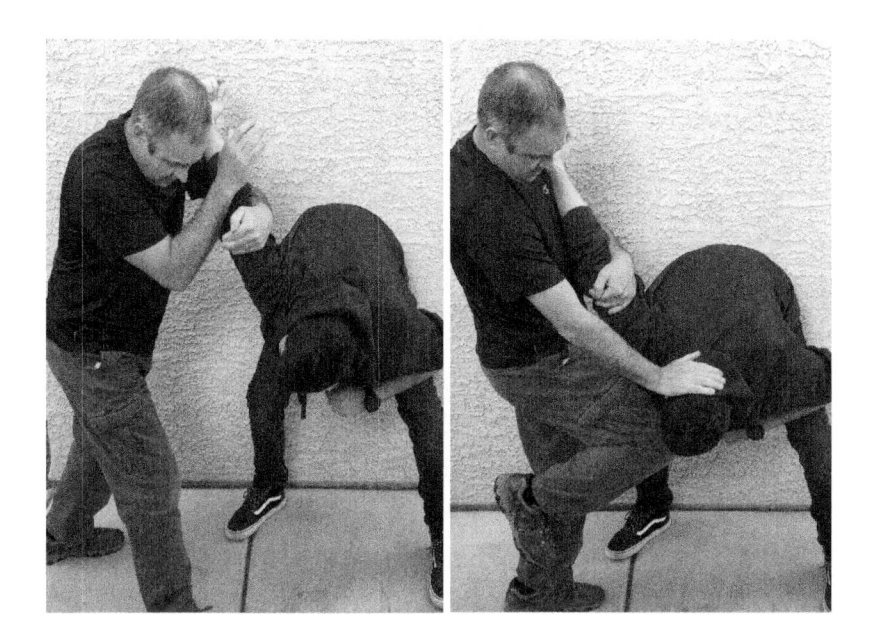

Reaction Without Thought

One of the most powerful skills a martial artist can possess is the ability to respond and react without conscious thought. Although this skill takes hard work to achieve, it is not unattainable. In fact, you may not realize it, but you already respond without conscious thought numerous times throughout your day.

Think of the last time someone threw a ball at you when you weren't paying attention. You probably caught the ball or at least deflected it without any thought whatsoever. You didn't take the time to think, "Oh, a ball is headed towards my face at a rapid speed, what shall I do?" You simply reacted with no conscious thought. How did this happen? There are two simple reasons that caused your instantaneous reaction.

First, you have probably caught a ball literally hundreds of thousands of times in your life. You probably played catch with your parents shortly after you were able to walk. You might have played ball games with neighborhood friends, on the school yard, and even in high school. Catching a ball is second nature to you because you have done it so many times. It is ingrained in your subconscious.

Second, the human mind has a process for responding to situations. Under normal conditions, it basically boils down to three steps that include, recognizing the situation is occurring, processing the information to determine the appropriate response, and reacting to the situation based on the response that was chosen. For routine situations, this process works fine, but during emergencies there is no time for the second step to occur, so your mind and body skip that step and respond unconsciously.

Imagine if your mind and body did not skip the second step during an emergency. You would always be too slow to respond to any threat that occurs. The human race would have literally died off thousands of years ago with primitive man being completely at the mercy of mammoths and saber tooth tigers. Imagine accidently touching a hot stove and your mind having to process the information and choose a response before you pulled your hand away. Skipping the second step in the process happens automatically, but it doesn't always guarantee the proper response happens.

Take the ball scenario again. This time, you are standing near the roadway when the ball is thrown at your face. You react instantly with no conscious thought by jumping out of the way of the incoming ball. The problem is you jump into the roadway, right into the path of an oncoming semi-truck. This is obviously not the best response, even though it was instantaneous and without thought.

In a time of crisis, your body will react in a manner that is consistent with how you have been programmed and conditioned throughout your life. This is why the old saying in martial arts and the military is so true, "How you train is how you fight". Through proper training, you can condition yourself to respond in a certain manner when serious situations occur, and the second step of the process is skipped.

The primary way to develop the ability to respond without thought is through repetition. This can not be mindless execution of techniques in the air. It has to be intense repetition under conditions that mimic a real situation. Your whole goal is to develop a proper response. When an attack occurs, the last thing you want your subconscious to pull out of the hat is a sloppy halfhearted response. The following exercise can be used to develop your unconscious response.

Response Without Thought Exercise One
Focused Repetition

To perform this exercise, choose a specific response you want to ingrain in your subconscious. Maybe it is a defense against a lead punch or a counter against a low kick. This technique will be the primary focus of your training for the next thirty days. You will use two methods during this time period to develop an unconscious response.

The first method of practice will be to have a training partner attack you as you perform the technique you have chosen. You should set a goal of at least two hundred repetitions a day, and practice with intensity as close to reality as possible. It is ok to take short breaks and do sets of fifty repetitions at a time, but you must remain focused and perform each repetition as perfectly as possible.

The second method will involve using visualization combined with repetitions of the technique in the air. This can be broken up into short segments that you do in between chores around the house, on a coffee break at work, or anytime that you have a minute to spare. Find a quiet place where you won't be disturbed and assume a fighting posture. Then vividly imagine an opponent attacking you as you actually perform repetitions of the technique in the air. Try to make this practice feel exactly the same as your practice with a partner did. Try to perform at least fifty repetitions at a time.

After thirty days of daily executing your technique two hundred repetitions with a partner, and one or two hundred repetitions in the air with visualization, it will start to become second nature to you. You should keep practicing the technique in your normal training sessions, but you can pick a new technique for the focused repetition exercise. Eventually, you will be sparring, or a situation will occur that triggers your conditioned response, and you will be surprised when your technique happens automatically without conscious thought.

I must emphasize one more time the importance of focus in this exercise. If you blindly execute your techniques and just go through the motions you will be wasting your time or worse yet, conditioning poor technique. You must focus on both your mental intent and your physical technique as you do each repetition. This is a true example of mind and body operating as one.

Just like the example of stepping in front of the truck to catch the ball, you should be aware of techniques the opponent might use to set you up and solicit a desired response from you. By paying attention to the attacker's body language, you can read what his next move might be and not get caught in this trap. When looking for indicators that determine your opponent's intentions, pay special attention to his eyes, shoulders, footwork, and hands. Let's break down some of the indicators for each one.

Eyes- The eyes are truly the window to the soul. Often the eyes betray a person's true intentions. Fighters will often telegraph their next move by looking at a target just prior to launching their attack. Pay attention to the eyes but remember that they can be used to mislead you as well. The age-old trick of looking at one target and then striking another fall into this category.

Shoulders- It is almost impossible to throw a powerful punch without using your shoulders. Inexperienced fighters will usually wind up and pull their shoulder back just before they punch. The shoulders don't move very fast compared to arms, legs, fists, and feet. This makes it easier to monitor them and stop attacks by jamming or checking the shoulder blades.

Footwork- The opponent's footwork will often indicate his intentions. If he is creating distance and placing all of his weight on one leg, he might be preparing to kick. If he is moving in and staying light on his feet, you can expect hand techniques are coming. A wider stance with open hands, and short inching footwork might indicate a takedown or grappling technique is coming. Footwork is similar to the tires on a work vehicle, the type of tire indicates the type of work being done. Does the vehicle have snow tires, large mud tires, or bald racing tires? The same holds true for a fighter's footwork.

Hands- There is a golden rule in law enforcement and self-defense that you must always watch a suspect's hands. The hands are literally what will kill you in an encounter. Hands held in a pocket or behind the back are probably concealing a weapon of some kind. If the opponent is making a tight fist, expect a punch is coming. If his hands are open, he will probably be looking to grab you.

Paying close attention to these indicators will prevent you from having your conditioned response triggered by a false attack. As a well-rounded fighter, you should also look at all of these concepts and see how you can potentially use them against your opponent. For example, you might clench a fist and look directly at the opponent's jaw to make him believe you intend to attack him there. Once his response is triggered, you strike another area where he is unprotected.

Remember that any martial arts concept or technique that you learn can be used both to protect you and also to harm your opponent. Make a habit of always looking at the coin from both sides.

Conclusion

When I look back over the more than four decades I have spent practicing and learning the martial arts, I think about the knowledge my teachers passed on to me that really opened my mind and took my skills to a new level. It was my sincere goal to pass on to you some of these ideas and concepts that I believe should be a part of all martial arts systems. If you take the time to really study the concepts presented in this book, and incorporate them into your own training, I am sure that you will see significant benefits in both your fighting skills and you daily life. I wish you a safe and successful journey!

Chuck Callaway
January 2021

About the Author

Chuck Callaway is a martial artist with over forty years of experience in the fighting arts. He holds black belts is several systems including, Tang Soo Do, Molum Combat Arts, and Filipino Arnis. He has trained extensively in Jiujitsu, Judo, Kung-Fu, Boxing, Kali, and Tai Chi. In 1987, he met Sifu Vic Butler who taught him the devastating art of elbow boxing, Goshin Budo Jiujitsu, and Molum Combat Arts. After years of intense training, Chuck earned his 3rd degree black belt from Sifu Butler. In addition to his study of traditional martial arts, Chuck received training in hand-to-hand combat and weapons skills while serving as a Security Police Specialist in the military. He was also a certified defensive tactics instructor for law enforcement and has taught martial arts to private students for decades. He continues his lifelong journey of learning and training in the martial arts.

Printed in Great Britain
by Amazon